MY NATIVE LAND SINGS TO ME

To: Carol
with many wishes!!
Nadia Steffi

St. Augustine

Oct. 18, 2018

About the Author: Nadia Steffè is retired and living in Florida with her husband. She has been recognized for her poetry and children's stories, which she wrote and illustrated and is available in electronic form. Over the years has been fortunate enough to reunite with family members who immigrated to Australia after WWII.

My Native Land Sings to Me

A Memoir

By

Nadia Steffè

My Native Land Sings to Me © 2018 Nadia Steffè. The poem "My Home" © 2018 Nadia Steffè. No part of this book may be reproduced in any manner whatsoever, including Internet usage without written permission from Nadia Steffè except in the case of brief quotations embodied in critical articles and reviews.

First Edition

Available from Amazon.com, CreateSpace.com, and other retail outlets

Cover design by Sabrina Della Penta

ISBN 13: 978-1718957688
ISBN 10: 1718957688

Dedication

Many times I have been asked, no, told to write "my story." Friends, family, people I have encountered in different places and times said they would love to read and learn of the many instances in this life of mine.

For Liselotte, who shared some time with me at Middlesex County College and entreated me to write this little bit of history as soon as possible.
For my colleagues and acquaintances who insisted I must write this story.
For the dear friends who were and are part of my life.
For the memory of my beloved mother, father and sister who rest in Mount Royal Cemetery, Montreal.
For my sister Bianca who still shares my life.
For my husband, Mario, whom I continue to love after these 52+ years.
For my daughters, my grandchildren and great grandchildren so they may know where they all started from and what, hopefully, helped shaped their own lives.

A long time ago in East Brunswick I worked with women some of whom loved to spend their free time reading every single issue of Hollywood gossip magazines. While we talked of many things among which were our lives—upon learning of the differences between their American conventional, ordinary (they claimed) days and some of my past experiences—some were eager to learn more about my ordinary life. One woman in particular said, "What, do you really think your life is so interesting and different than ours?"

To her, and all women who are blessed to have been born, live and grow up in this USA, I especially dedicate this short story. Perhaps you will remember and think about me any and every time you hear or talk about or to an immigrant for many of their lives are parallel to mine.

Contents

My Home xiv
Illustration of Italy Post-WWII xix
Book One—Italia 1
- I 3
- II 8
- III 12
- IV 14
- V 18

Book Two—Canada 23
- I 25
- II 27
- III 29
- IV 32
- V 40
- VI 46
- VII 49
- VIII 52
- IX 58
- X 67

Book Three—The United States 107
- I 109
- II 110
- III 112
- IV 117
- V 119
- VI 122
- VII 126
- VIII 127
- IX 132
- X 135
- XI 139
- XII 144

XIII 150
XIV 154

My Home

Far away in time and place lies a piece of land that by divine grace was once my home; my native land.
Green and fertile were her hills. The valleys where my ancestors tilled
ample food supplied for its native brood.
The sea unto which it juts was blue-green unpolluted teeming with fish.

Istria, my home, my native land!

Men and women of varied skin-tones sang and prayed in different tongues.
Yet for a time lived and died in harmony and without strife.
But inch by inch and year by year, men of power, men of will,
Let greed and differences grow till with diffidence and hate hearts grew cold;
Smiles faded, tears began to fall.

War!...O, that dreaded word, took hold!

Army boots marched where peasants' feet did thread! The songs of that place bombs replaced! Ditches with mangled bodies filled! Ropes hanged the innocent even our priest!
Farmland stood parched, in the fear! Partisans hid in the green hills!
Neighbors and friends no longer shared! Brother for brother no longer cared!

Young wives hugged tight at their good-byes! Fathers would never see their newborns' eyes! Mothers . . . their sorrow only another mother could know.

Cain and Abel desecrating the Holiest anew.

Lord . . . Why did your hand not stem the kill? Where were you God those terrible years?!
Hiding your face from all that slaughter brought onto and by your sons and daughters!
Homes that once held ones so dear, full of suffering, full of tears! Many houses empty stood for days on end! Many people their homeland fled!

Others, once *neighbors*, now *enemies*, took their place!

Far across the ocean wide my family did travel in those days of strife.
How will it be? What will we find? Why did the fate so hard hit our life?
With anguish, fear and hope inside, Love for each other and only Faith to guide;
Refugee camp and a long wait. A fearful trip across winter weather strewn waves.
Onto shore of a strange far away land did the five of us wander a new life to find.

"What is all that white stuff, mamma?" A young child, I asked in awe.

"Why snow, piccola mia," she whispered near. So much of it we'd never seen!
Back home by now April flowers bloomed. But here they tell us winter still loomed.
Kind hearted people warm coats provide. Some warmer shoes and boots we'd find.

Papà, Mamma and older sister too all took any job that they could do
To feed and clothe and keep us safe from harm.

When will we again embrace grandparents, uncles, aunts?

Oh, to walk on our childhood shores once more. To cool in the waves of our blessed sea.
That now holds captive in its deep bodies of sailors in their sunken ships.
We'll make a new and better life. We'll hide the pain; roll up our sleeves.
New friendship will form out of common grief. New neighbors' prejudice we will breach,
Even as our hearts still weep for mothers, brothers, friends and green hills.

Love for our new host country we will learn and teach.

The years have passed. We're older, wiser and yet our hearts still ache;
On days when thoughts wander far away across the sea to another land that once was free.
Dear ones now gone, without one last good-by. Bitter that pill!
Those letters that told of their demise. Our souls were gashed to bits! . . . Life demands we go on and live.
Throats knot as in books we read; Sir Walter Scott knew our souls even in time of yore;

"Lives there the man with soul so dead
That never to himself has said,
This is my home my native land."

As days went by we tried to assimilate. We learned new languages new ways.

But it's not easy to forget what you learned on father's knee.
American-European what should I be?
A teenager already has his/her struggles to bear, without the identity crisis to share.
"Don't forget what you are," Papà would say. "Look to the future!" entreated friends.

Torment and struggle within my heart! Would these years ever pass?!

Souvenirs haunt the dreams of those whose hearts still long.
Have songs returned to those ravaged hills? Can you hear the children's gay shrills?
Is my native land now your homeland? Love it, please, as once I did.
Keep it now safe from hate and greed. No more to shed innocent blood;
No more the sorrow; the fear; the longing for the land so dear.

In its sharing, God brethren made us of His divine will.

I found a love beautiful and new. Together a home we built, we two.
We labored each day in this bountiful land. Yes our life was grand!
Children I bore, together we've grown a new family in a new home.
We did go back to that far away land. In trepidation we walked hand in hand.
But the singing was gone, the buildings bare, the children hid as we neared.

Our loved ones no longer here. Some are dead. Some gone elsewhere.

The house that once my home I called! Someone else now lives there.
I cannot converse for they speak a different tongue, I smile shyly and turn around.

The school where I first learned to read and write. The church where I saw my mother cry
The day we left this land so dear; was it long ago? Or yesteryear.
We board the plane, I hold his hand. He kisses my lips tenderly and wipes a tear.

"We're home, we're here," He shakes me awake.

I leave behind all the old dreams. The memories however live with me still.
In sorrow we buried our parents dear, their souls to God commending here.
Fate brought me to these distant shores. Who knows for what! Must I do more?!
Kindness and tolerance I'll preach. Pain will perhaps ease
When we each learn this grain of sand called EARTH, to proudly defend as God's gift;

"Our Home Our Native Land"

By Nadia Steffè

Illustration of Italy Post-WWII*

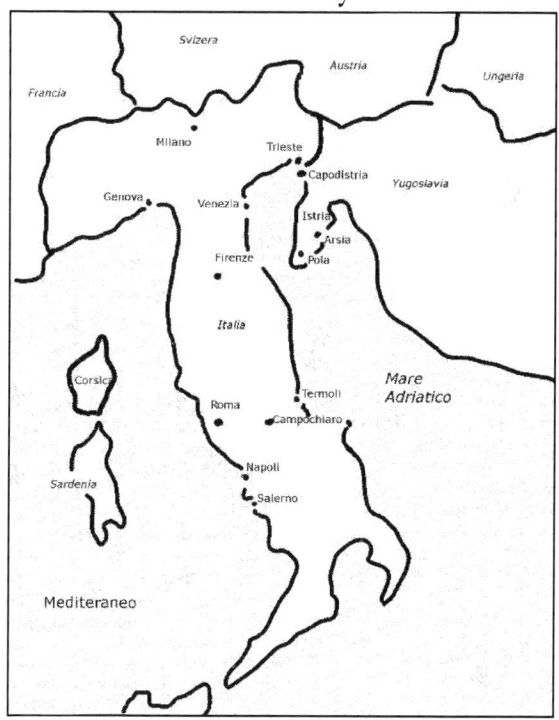

*Not to scale

Book One—Italia

I

Mio Papà (my father), Giovanni Steffè, came from a very large family. He was number 19 of 21 or 24 children; the actual number still in discussion among cousins. There were at least two sets of twins. His mother, Margarita, a strapping farmer's wife. His father, Antonio, tall, strong and with dark brown eyes and black hair, was a horticulturalist and owned a lot of farmland in Santa Domenica d'Albona on the eastern side of the Istrian peninsula jutting out into the northern part of the Adriatic Sea: Venice to the west and Istria to the east. Nonno and Nonna (grandfather and grandmother) were of Italian descent, but lived under Austrian-Hungarian rule. During World War I, Nonno Antonio had been hired by the government to augment the production of food with which to feed the military. Meanwhile Papà and a sister—they were two of the youngest siblings—were sent to live on a Hungarian family's farm further inland; they would be safer there. He told us how very often their meals consisted of only two walnuts and a piece of bread or a turnip and some bread.

After 1918, when Istria was forfeited by the Hapsburgs to Italy, the family continued to work Nonno's farms. It was expected the sons would continue the farming tradition, but as they grew up, not all wanted to work the land. Eventually, the two eldest sons got their father drunk and tricked him into signing deeds of sale to a large part of his property. Once sober, Nonno realized what happened and right there and then had a deadly heart attack.

With the new found riches from their inherited proceeds of the sales, my uncles purchased a large building in the city in which they lived. They ran a trucking company and were among the first men in that territory to own not only trucks, but cars and motorcycles . . . as well as the rest of the land. At 14 Papà was already one of their mechanics and truck drivers. He told us how they had to learn to make working pieces from broken parts to repair their trucks. Told us about some of the places he drove those trucks. How they were hired to transport the ore from the bauxite mines in Albona and coal from Arsia (now part of Croatia). Of the beautiful caves with wonderful stalactites and stalagmites he felt privileged to visit in Postumia (70 miles north into modern-day Slovenia). Eventually, he also brought his cousin Gisella, later to be his wife, there. Yes, mom and dad were second cousins with the same last name.

Mamma was a beautiful girl, about five feet six inches tall, with traits one often thinks of as Austrian: fair skin, blue eyes and blond hair, probably inherited from her mother's family, whose last name was Starz. With mio papà standing at five feet ten inches, with very large, strong hands, black hair that never, even in his 70s, turned gray, and dark brown eyes, they most surely made a good-looking couple. They fell deeply in love. The priest did not want to marry them when they appeared before him. Mamma, age 22, was already pregnant, so father told him, "Fine, we will live in sin together anyway." The priest relented and they married. It was fall of 1934. Their first daughter, my oldest sister Giuliana, was born in Santa Domenica, district of Albona, in February 1935.

Because of its strategic position, Istria, with its different ports on the Adriatic, has been coveted by many and fought over many times. After a short period of peace the region found itself again at war. In 1939 Germany, on the move to conquer, slowly crept upon our area. World War II broke the family apart with some zias and zios (aunts and uncles) moving their families to safety in different directions. The partners sold some property and moved 70 miles north to Trieste, a ship-building, coastal city, where they believed they would be safer. At Capodistria, one of the other larger cities on the Adriatic coast a few miles south of Trieste and my maternal family home, Zio Natale purchased an osteria (family restaurant). Papà told us of his anger after seeing his rich brothers actually lighting cigars with rolled up wads of money, while the younger family members received very little compensation for their work!

During the war families were moved inland from the Adriatic whose coastal cities, especially Trieste, a major ship-building port, were always in danger of attack. That is how my sister Bianca and I were born in Canfanaro in the province of Pola in 1941 and 1943 respectively. Later we moved to Capodistria where mamma's parents still lived. It was not really much safer of an area. The Germans were retreating, leaving behind the destruction of war. Italians were themselves divided among the pro-Re Vittorio Emanuele III (king of Italy) factions and Prime Minister Benito Mussolini-led fascists. The Slavs, who were led by the socialist party and nursing old hatreds of Italians predating WWI—and were then part of the Allied Forces—began guerrilla warfare to take over the ports. The Slavic and Italian partisans were at each other's throats, very often literally.

Some of my family members were lost to the chaos, including one of the twin uncles who was killed for refusing to repair a small plane belonging to some Slavic men—he was never seen again. His wife became a nuisance begging everyone to know where his body was that she may bury him properly. She too was murdered. Masked men with guns entered her house while she was resting in bed, a female friend visiting her for comfort. My two frightened young cousins, seven and three years old, hid under their mamma's bed. The men and women argued. Somehow one of the masks was pulled off and my zia recognized the intruder and yelled out his name. The two young ladies were shot. After the men left, my cousins crawled out of hiding to find their friend dead and their mamma conscious but bleeding badly. The seven-year-old was told to fetch a neighbor. Her toddler brother scampered on his mother's arms and was found covered in blood hugging his mamma. The family always believed that this atrocity had much to do with the seven-year-old's mental instability in later years.

It was also during this time that the Slavic partisans committed the most horrific acts. Many who objected to their ideals and the confiscation of their lands were killed. Many men, young and old, were made to dig ditches and then either were tied together in rows or simply made to stand in line next to the holes—BANG BANG BANG—they were shot and fell in the ditches they had been forced to dig. Some of those people were still alive when they were covered with dirt. The peninsula also provided natural crevasses and sinkholes in which bodies were disposed in. These are the Foibe that are still being explored for the human remains they contain. For a long time after the war Italy refused to hear the plight of the families of these poor creatures. Unlike the Jews who stood for "We shall never forget," the post-war Italians, defeated by the allies, liberated from German occupation, stripped of territory and not yet unified in government, did not want to ruffle any feathers. It was not until 60 years later on February 10, 2005 that a day of remembrance was established and the Italian government honored 15,000 murdered men, women and children that they recognized at the time.

II

I was about five when my first actual, personal memory of war came to be. My sisters and I were playing at a friend's house. The house was on a little cliff over a stretch of beach on the Adriatic which from Roman times had been used for the mining of salt, mainly for local consumption. There were wooden boxes laid out on the beach, and as the sea tide rose and fell, shallow water would be caught in these instead of ebbing out to sea. The sun would evaporate the water leaving the salt deposits behind. The bottom of the Mediterranean Sea, as well as the waters that made up the Adriatic, was historically heavy with salt deposits that began millions of years ago when the Strait of Gibraltar was not yet formed.

It was such a lovely sunny day—we always loved playing near the sea; that was so much a part of our communal life—we went outside to play, with Giuliana for supervision of course. My friend and I were playing, holding hands as we skipped along, singing one of the many children's songs we loved, when we came upon a deep hole. Just an ordinary hole with dirt sides going down maybe two feet or so. Excited by the playtime, curious and adventurous, holding hands, we stood on the rim of the hole ready to jump in—suddenly, strong hands grabbed us by our dress collars and yanked us backwards. I was close to choking as I landed on my butt.

"Hey, why did you pull us?!"

Thanks to the attentiveness of my 13-year-old sister we were saved. On the bottom of the hole laid an un-exploded device left over from the bombing. We ran back home and were hugged and held tight by our mothers as Giuliana told of the find. Thank God for big sisters! The shore by our beloved sea held some deep and ugly dangers. It was also just by Capodistria that the Italian ocean liner the SS Rex was hit by Royal Air Force (RAF) on September 8, 1944. My parents remembered it burning for four days before it finally settled in shallow water.

The next few years were unsettled for the adults but for us children they were for the most part happy years. We were all together, lived near loving relatives, had plenty of space to play in the safe streets and nearby piazzas, and enjoyed the simple life there. In the mornings we would hear the chatter of neighbors, the singing of songs as women went about their chores. The schools were nearby and the time passed easily for us.

I was a delicate child. Because of a heart murmur I had been diagnosed with since birth, I was expected to be a weakling my whole life. So as the youngest and in a weak condition I was spoiled by the rest of the family. The best cut of meat, the freshest milk to drink, the best of the fruits were mine. In the spring of 1949 and then again in 1950, I was sent to a government-subsidized camp up in the mountains for my health. It was called Enego and located at Candide di Candore in the Province of Vicenza, the Veneto region of Italy, approximately 99.5 miles from home. The mountains with the thick pine forests were believed to be very healthy and beneficial. I enjoyed the mountains and the outings in the pine groves that were part of the campsite. During the day we attended classes taught mostly by nuns, who of course taught us our Catechism as we were of the age to prepare for First Communion.

During Holy Week I was in the infirmary with perhaps just a cold, I do not exactly recall. I do remember that in the evening, after lights out for the children, I saw the young nurses at the lighted nurse station eating the chocolate Easter egg my parents had sent for me. I secretly hoped they would choke on the chocolate! The Italian tradition at Easter is to give children hollow egg-shaped chocolate of various sizes with a surprise inside, usually a small toy, perhaps a little wooden car or a ring or necklace. There were, and still are, even bigger eggs with things for adults such as a little coffee cup or silver spoon for espresso coffee. The eggs were always wrapped in colorful paper, tied with big, beautiful bows. No Easter egg for me!

After two days in the infirmary I was able to go back to my dorm room. Then the day after I was reprimanded by the nun in charge of my room. Apparently while I was in the infirmary, someone had told the little girl in the bed next to mine that her parents had come to take her sister home, but she had to remain until she was well again. She had cried so much she made herself sicker. The nun described the girl that blabbed as wearing a black smock with a white bow on the collar, which is what I wore every day, but so did about a hundred other girls! Smocks and bows: it was and still is a customary dress for young children, especially in kindergarten and elementary grades. The clothes we wore underneath remained clean even during playtime and arts and crafts especially. Clothes were expensive, and washing clothes in those early years with no washing machine was too demanding in both time and labor. The smock we wore as a school uniform took care of all that.

    That evening when it was time for bed, during our walk in single file to the last restroom trip before sleep, the nun in charge refused to hand me my ration of toilet paper—two sheets of soft paper, maybe four by five inches in size—and so I forced my body not to poop. I just urinated and went to bed. Of course, nature is stronger than our will, especially at that young age. I was humiliated again in the morning when I was found with a soiled bed and made the laughing stock of the dorm. A young priest who helped with our Catechism lessons heard my confession as a practice run and then told the sisters that I had indeed told the truth, I was not the one who blabbed. How could I have been the one who told? In the infirmary one did not ever wear the smock used for school time, but a special cover-up. The nuns gave me an extra cookie at lunchtime, no apologies just a cookie. The bitterness stayed with me however. I did not like nuns much after that. Before it was time for our big day of our First Communion Feast, my parents came to pick me up from camp.

III

Many Italian locals wanted to leave Istria which was now run by Joseph B. Tito's Socialist Yugoslavian army, but they were not allowed to take anything of value with them. Papà, now working as a truck driver for the local co-operative of Capositria, had been asked by a couple of wealthier folks to secretly bring their money to the Territorio Libero di Trieste (Free Territory of Trieste) which was under the protective umbrella of the United Nations. But Papà was afraid of what could happen to him, as well as his family, if he had been stopped and contraband material found in his truck. For a few days we did not see him. Later, we found out he had been hiding in my grandparent's house and then under an old mattress in our attic. We were told he was playing hide-and-seek, but we did not understand who the other players were.

We moved from Capodistria to Trieste where, with two other relative families, we bunked at Zio Nat's home. I remember our sleeping arrangements: in a not-so-large bed my oldest sister and two girl cousins slept at the head of the bed, while Bianca and I shared the space at their feet. So with the owners of the house and restaurant (Zio now owned a new osteria which abutted the house) we were four families in that one house.

To get from the sleeping quarters to the restaurant area you went down a step and across a very narrow lane to the door that opened onto the business area. One morning I woke up with a very swollen eyelid. Zia Natalia recognized it as a spider bite. Even though uncomfortable, I sat on the step and laughed as she ran after the spider with one slipper on her foot and one in her hand until she was satisfied she had killed the culprit, a daddy long-legs.

Papà tried to find work in Trieste. The osteria was not busy enough to warrant more help. A widowed sister of his owned a newsstand that she hired someone else to run. Papà asked her to let him run it, but she said no. She had worked with that man for many years and thought that my father did not have the experience to run the small enterprise. In later years, we thought that perhaps there was more to the relationship between Zia and the newsman. He continued his search for employment as many, many more people were crowding into the free city as they were leaving Tito's totalitarian rule. Jobs were scarce after the war and willing, needy hands too many. Time went by slowly.

I started third grade, Bianca her fourth, in Trieste. Giuliana was in the liceo (high school). Bianca and I walked together to school in the mornings and always passed a house in which a pet Capuchin monkey sat on the window sill while its owner stood behind it. It waved to us by placing its right arm under its hind right leg. This always made us laugh, and we went that way each day happy to see that Capuchin monkey wave, and we waved back. We did not finish our school year there however; we had to begin our odyssey.

IV

In July of 1945 President Harry S. Truman appeared at the Postdam Conference, a suburb of Berlin, attended also by Prime Minister Winston Churchill and Soviet Premier Joseph Stalin. These allies set the boundaries of the war-torn parts of our lands. Much of Istria was allotted to Tito who favored the communism of the Russians. Our land was not ours any longer! Even the farms worked every day for whole lives by my relatives now belonged to the new government and the old owners were told how to manage and run them all for the benefit of the "whole and not for the personal." How much of the produce would be taken by the leaders and how little would remain for the working families?

Like many others who did not want to live under the Slavic State and Communist party, my parents decided to leave. In 1950 we became part of the Istrian Exodus. The refugees from those lands were many, and Italy and other European countries devastated by years of horrible war had little, if anything at all, to offer to these new transplanted people.

Finally the United Nations and the Allies granted permission for people from the region through the International Refugee Organization (IRO) to emigrate to a free country. Four countries were accepting refugees from our area: Argentina, Australia, Canada and the United States. Our extended family was sparse and those who wanted started the process of leaving. One of our young adult male cousins wanted to get to United States, a country he knew from the movies and the many US soldiers he came in contact with in Trieste. With my parents' promises of looking after him his family granted him their blessings.

Our new adventure started that fall. From Trieste we took a train to southern Italy where a camp had been set up for the first part of the process. At the displaced person's camp, DP Camp Bagnoli, Naples, we were first health screened—probed, x-rayed, vaccinated—and put on the list of people wanting to emigrate. Once that process done, my parents took some time to visit one of my mother's cousins living in the Margellina section of Naples. I don't have other memories from there except for standing on a large terrace with a most beautiful view of the city, the port of Naples and the bluest sea I had ever seen. Although we had lived practically on the Adriatic, this water expanse seemed much wider than our local sea. We were up on a hill, so the view went out all the way to the nearby islands, Ischia and even Capri. The whole family enjoyed the stay there and the beautiful views, but it was a short visit.

Soon we returned to Capodistria to gather the little belongings we were allowed to bring with us. It was sad to say goodbye to our nonna, our zia, who was also my godmother, and the two zios who would remain behind. We had lived for years so near to them and we loved them so much. Then we were off to Trieste to say our goodbyes to the rest of the relatives. My paternal nonna, at least six zias and zios and a few cousins. If I close my eyes I can relive the scene at the train station: me, now seven, holding a sawdust-stuffed white Siamese cat and Bianca, now nine, carrying two books, for me Senza Calce e Senza Soldi (Without Lime and Without Money), which is to this day on my bookshelf, and Bianca's storybook about hens and roosters, whose title I don't recall—going away presents from our aunts; Giuliana, at 15, crying as she held tight to the friends and cousins who accompanied us to the train station; our cousin who was coming with us excitedly talking to his family and friends; and my parents trying desperately to hold back the tears as they said their adios. They knew even then how difficult it would be to ever see their parents, sisters, brothers again.

The train stopped under the canopy in the large train station. I held that white cat tight to my chest as our meager belongings were put on the train compartment that we were to inhabit during this trip: a couple of bags for the immediate necessities and two wooden trunks of modest size that held the few belongings we were allowed to bring with us. Mamma had packed some clothing, bed linens, covers for the expected colder climate we were to find in our new home. Among these things a prized aluminum pot in which mother could cook anything, from the soups my father loved to the stews that made up our regular fare back home.

It is 781.6 miles from Trieste to our destination in Germany. At the time and with the old trains it must have taken at least 14 hours to get there. Don't have much recollection of the train trip itself, perhaps it was night. I do remember laying down with my head on mamma's lap to sleep.

Finally the train arrived at its destination in Lesum, Germany. We along with other families were put on a truck with our belongings and were driven to another DP Camp. I remember the Camp as a group of what had been soldiers' barracks, a very clean, austere environment. We were greeted kindly by personnel of the IRO, fed and then showed to our quarters. Men slept in one barrack, women and children in another. Bottom part of bunk beds draped by top sheets were used as dressing and changing areas by the most shy of ladies, like my most modest mother. We would be together during the day and all ate in the mess hall. When not required to answer the never-ending questions from the staff, the grownups would pass their free time mostly in card games and letter writing. We younger children played in the small playground where

I remember swinging too high on the swing set. I flew off and ended up with a nosebleed. While my sister ran for help, a young boy named Mario whom we had befriended handed me his handkerchief. From that day he became my best friend and remained so until after I married. The odd thing, his name is the same as my husband's . . . coincidence?

Christmastime custom back home included giving toys to children on December 6, the Feast of St. Nicholas, who brought gifts to poor children. Somehow my parents managed a little gift for us younger sisters to share. I can cup my hands and still feel the round, rubber yellow ball with its vibrant blue and red stripes. What a jewel that was! And as other children left for their destinations, they would sometimes give away what they no longer wanted. I loved the book of fairy tales I received, and my sister had been given a celluloid doll whose face had been scorched in wartime but was still, o, so beautiful to us. Those simple objects were our treasures for many years to come

V

Our migration in action again, the list of names next in line to leave the camp came to our family's. Our cousin was granted passage to the US, but after his name, the quota to the US was met—my father would not be allowed to join him. What a big disappointment! The question was whether to let him move on, on his own or have him return home to Italy. I can imagine, now as a parent, what that would have cost him, his parents and my parents as well. It was decided, then, that my immediate family would opt for Canada, since it seemed more probable that we should see each other again from there rather than from Australia, where our other aunts and uncle and their broods had gone to (some of whom we missed meeting in Lesum only by two days).

Papà sailed in mid-December of 1950 on a ship that had been converted from cargo to migrant passage by the name of Fairsea. MS Fairsea along with other ships like her traveled from European ports with their cargo of migrants to the four countries accepting them. I do not recall going to the port to see Papà off. It was better to say our farewells at the camp, that way the women and children would not be too upset or make a ruckus. My mother seemed very sad after Papà left, but she did her best to keep us happy. The voyage was long and treacherous, and many a woman cried upon receiving news that a ship traveling to Canada had been sunk in bad weather. The struggle showed on our mother's face until the happy day, a whole month later, when news arrived of that ship's safe landing in Halifax, Nova Scotia.

Many years later in New Jersey, US, I woke from a nap on my sofa to a PBS program close to ending but enough to hear that they were showing the trial of the captain of the Fairsea. He had refused to go to the help of a cargo ship that was in dire danger. His reasoning: he had a cargo full of human souls and was just as likely to be sunk in that horrible weather if he backtracked to help. Under the circumstances and deliberation by the court he was fully absolved. I tried to find that PBS program in vain for years after but was happy to at least be able to relate to my family that information.

  Our young cousin had been lucky upon his arrival to the USA and was settled and found good employment in Missouri, and dad and he had been in contact. It was a loan from him of $100 dollars (like a million would be to us today) that allowed my father to pay someone to move the rest of us up on the list for transfer to Canada. Our trip across the Atlantic that March on the MS Skaubryn, a Norwegian passenger ship, was not an easy one either. I recall one day, while the grownups played cards and we young ones entertained ourselves, the ocean had gotten very rough: waves came in one side of the mess hall windows and out the other side. The tables were bolted to the floors I suppose for just such a reason. Personally I was seasick most of the time. My sisters fared better, especially Giuliana who with her teen friends helped care for the feeble persons. Bianca was also of help to me and to Mamma. Many an adult were covered and strapped to the chairs on the decks in rough waters when they refused to go below. As much as I always like the sea, the ocean voyage was painful for me. We arrived in Halifax on April 1, 1951. Happy Fools Day!

Book Two—Canada

I

I recall holding hands with Bianca as we walked down the plank. It was way up high and the dock and the water waaaay down below; of course, we were small then and all else, as our ship, seemed monumental. Anticipation and fear co-mingled in our hearts as we slowly, tentatively made our way to terra ferma. Our innards were still doing the waving motion of the ocean. It took some time for our bodies, hearts and souls to settle into firm stance.

We were happy to finally arrive in Canada, but it was bitterly cold. Our light coats were hardly fit for Canadian winters. Church members helped us with the re-registration process and were kind enough to provide us with warmer coats, hats, gloves and the very necessary galoshes. Bless them still.

Soon we were on a train again. During this trip I was much more aware. In Halifax it had been cold, but the weather was mitigated by the ocean air. Now as we neared the interior of the province of Quebec all the views were white. I asked my mother what that was.

"Neve, piccola mia" (snow, my little one).

We did see snow back in Italy, but in our hometowns it rarely reached, and even less often, stayed on the ground. Here it covered everything:

streets, houses, vehicles and even the tall trees. We were glad we had the new coats and especially the galoshes.

This train brought us to DP Camp #3, St. Paul l'Ermite in the province of Quebec. There, families waited for a chance to find work which was the requisite for leaving the camp, unless one had family already able to help. More barracks, more strange foods, lots of Bologna cold cuts sandwiches. After a month or so of that the teenagers rebelled and the baloney from our lunches hung up on all the light shades around the mess hall. What a site as they sang and danced around with the sandwiches! My oldest sister among the leaders of the group. She was such a lively ball of fire.

One day a rich man came to look for workers for his estate. Much impressed with my father's mechanical and driving history hired him on the spot. So the whole family moved to Montebello, the estate of, as we knew him, Monsieur de Notembar, a descendant from a noble European family. In one swoop he hired his chauffeur, papà; a maid, my oldest sister; and a gatekeeper, mamma—us younger girls went along for the ride, as you would say. We were housed at the gatekeeper's comfortable cottage.

II

For the next six months dad drove the family wherever they wanted to go and picked up their visitors from the airports. People visited from many parts of the world. Montebello is approximately 50 miles east from Ottawa, Canada's capital city, just over the river, and dignitaries who came to visit Ottawa would often be guests at the chateau. Giuliana was a big help to the owners for she had already learned French at the liceo back home. Mother was eager to please and also helped out at the chateau. Papà, used to being his own person, fumed at the idea of his wife and daughter being servants. And he was especially mortified one Sunday, after he drove Monsieur et Madame to church, when he dared to kneel in the pew just behind them and he was told to leave in no uncertain terms by an usher. That pew belonged to another notable family. Their name was inscribed on a plaque set in the pew. We were not used to people owning a place in God's house. Papà taught us always that people were all the same and we all had the same place in Christ's heart. He was so hurt to be told how much lower he ranked in these people's eyes. It took him years to recover from the affront and to get his pride back before he stepped again in a church.

The estate was huge and comprised a lot of farmland. The Canadian farmers taught our father how to dig up potatoes, scrub them clean and eat them raw. We had never heard of eating raw potatoes, but Papà said fresh from the ground they were quite good. On Sunday afternoons we would go to the creek on the property and pan for gold as our friends had shown us. We saw some glitters but never found gold nuggets. It was said the mountain which bordered the estate had housed a working mine in the past. That summer the workers finished building a chapel on the grounds. The bishop came to bless the little church, and on that occasion I, in the floor-length white dress and veil that Bianca had used before me in Trieste, made my First Communion. My present from Monsieur et Madame for that occasion was a plastic, five-inch statuette of Jesus as King of the World.

  The addition to the household of the little pup Diana, a pretty cocker spaniel, enlivened our time. Bianca and I were in school learning French every day. It was a small cabin, one room for all grades. I do not rightly recall, but I guess from grade one to six, as was the custom in Canada then. My parents were horrified the day we came home angry that the young girl who was our teacher asked if Italy was a large village. I think that was partly what made my father want to leave Montebello. We had friends whom we contacted in Montreal, and with their encouragement we piled onto another truck and our farmer friends drove us the 80-plus miles east to Montreal, a large island in the St. Lawrence River. Sadly, we had to leave Diana behind not knowing what we should find in the big city.

III

I remember meeting with friends, especially my best friend Mario from the DP camp in Lesum. I was very happy to see that we would be living in the same city. Here the Church was the main hand ready to help the immigrants. We were directed to the Sons of Italy Club by the Italian priests. They helped immigrants, first of all, to find lodgings. Our first place in the city was an apartment-sharing arrangement with an old gentleman but only for a couple of weeks till better accommodations could be found. From there we moved to an apartment in the Jewish section of town where I made friends with Barbra from across the street and learned more English, mostly by watching children programs with Barbra on her TV. There we learned more about Jewish customs and, of course, their cuisine. We loved the pastrami and corned beef from the neighborhood butcher and the pickles in the barrels at his front door.

One day we were having lunch when we heard terrible screams coming from across the street. An older neighbor ran out of her apartment with her clothes in flames. She had been cleaning her wooden floors with gasoline — a common practice at the time — while smoking a cigarette. A spark set the gasoline on fire. My father and another neighbor ran to her with some bed covers to smother the fire out while we called the police. I will never forget those screams. To this day I cringe with every firefighter's truck that goes by and always say a prayer for the people involved. Shortly after that we moved again. This time to an apartment in what is now called Old Montreal, an exclusive area of downtown Montreal. Then, it was just cheaply rented apartments in old row houses. Some friends who had crossed the Atlantic with us and other newly arrived immigrants lived there. With the easy rents came the mice, the creaky floors, and in our particular rooms, the smell of rising fumes from the cleaning business from the floor below us. No use complaining to the landlords, after all, we were grateful to have a roof over our heads!

The family had gotten into a routine. On Saturdays, Papà and Mamma would do the weekly shopping, while we three sisters did our chores. Giuliana would take care of things like paying bills, etc. Bianca and I were to do the housecleaning. I would let Bianca sleep in as I waxed the hardwood floor, as long as she was up in time to cook lunch (mostly soups that my parents liked). I did not care for cooking then at all. Our new lives looked promising. My father found work with a steel construction firm belonging to an Italo-Canadian family. My mother and big sister were sewing in a clothes factory. Bianca and I attended school, and for the third time I found myself in third grade. Mr. Hawk's Third Grade was where the immigrants were placed no matter what your age or grade you should be in. As long as you reached his class by Christmas, you were speaking English well by the end of the school year. Our Lady of Mont Royal School was a school full of immigrants from Asia and many countries of Europe: Germans, Poles, Hungarians, Irish, Italians. And so, by hook or by crook, we learned English, some by receiving not a few cracked pointers on their heads and rulers slaps on their palms. I wonder why other places have dual-speaking classes. From what I hear and see, it is a way of keeping the immigrant as subgrade citizens. The schooling time and thus the language learning is cut in half. It takes much longer to learn a language when not fully immersed in it. In Montreal, children of different countries had schools in their language that they, as we, attended on Saturdays or weeknights after our regular English school. So we learned the new and also kept up with our mother tongues. This system was a very good thing for it allowed people to feel happy by keeping their individual culture, language and customs, as well as immersing in the new language. In turn, we kept in contact with our relatives in Italy and helped with our parent's assimilation in the new country. With the English and the French, that was also taught in Montreal's schools, we soon became fluent in three languages.

One Saturday, while our parents were out on their usual shopping trip, a letter came with the return address of our aunt in Italy. Giuliana opened the letter anxious for news from back home, but it was not happy news. The letter told of the death of our beloved Nonna Piccia (small grandmother) our mother's mother, so called for her small stature next to our Nonna Grande (our much taller father's mother). It broke our hearts, and we were unsure how to break the news and let Mamma read the letter. I was so heartbroken by the news I cried so much I ended up in bed with a fever. Nonna Piccia was 87 years old, and still she went to work the farm every morning by horse-drawn cart. Her husband lived during the week at the farm in their little farmhouse to protect the farm from looters. He followed his wife to heaven within three months. Papà's mother, Nonna Grande, died within a year also. She had lived to be 92, and it is said she died with all her teeth in her mouth that is how healthy and strong a woman she was. Those were the saddest times, without so much as being able to say our last farewells to those relatives we loved so much.

IV

The next three years passed with busy lives for all: school, work, new friends. Giuliana, now 20, had became engaged to a nice Italian boy and was so very happy. My parents were thrilled that she had found a good man to marry. I, on the other hand, was often sullen because of the heart murmur diagnosis that branded me a weakling. Rough sports were prohibited — I wasn't even taught to ride a bike. I roller skated but got tired easily. I would come home from school tired and just want to sleep.

We were in fifth grade. I was doing very well in school, whereas Bianca hated school; in fact, this was to be her last year. She was older, of course, than most girls in the class — she lost a good two-plus years in the move from one country to the other. But I loved school, books, and the friends I made there. Bianca just dreamed of going to work and earning money, and so she did the next year. She joined my mother and older sister in the factory.

Happy times came to a rude stop though, especially for me and my oldest sister. Early in spring of 1955 I felt more and more tired each day. One night I started to cough and woke up the whole house. My poor mother was horrified when she turned on the light in my room to see what was happening to me — I was coughing up blood. My pillow blood-stained, I shook with fright as I looked at the red sputum that was in my hands which I had held against my mouth. It took a while for my parents to calm me, the cough to subside, washing my hands and face, changing the bed sheets and pillow, and everyone getting back to sleep. The school doctor we saw the next morning said I must have coughed too hard and broke a blood vessel.

"Nothing to worry about," he said.

The next night it happened again. It was so close to the losses of our grandparents in Italy; secretly I thought I was dying and prayed to God, thanking him it was me and not someone else in the family who would die. Exhausted from the coughing, I finally fell asleep that second night holding tight to the rosary I was given way back in Halifax by the good sisters who provided us with warm clothing for the Canadian winters.

When it happened again for the third time, I was brought to a neighborhood clinic right then in the middle of the night. The doctor just tapped two of his fingers of one hand with one on his other hand on my chest and back. After talking very briefly to my parents and making them listen to the sound from my lungs as he tapped my back, he directly called for the emergency services and sent me to the nearest hospital. TB was a scary term — mamma was both angry at the first doctor and relieved to have found this one, Doctor Longtin.

"One more hemorrhage like that and you would have lost her."

The whole family was tested and Giuliana was also found to be ill. Funny that Bianca with whom I shared a bedroom had not caught the illness. Giuliana had probably not gotten it directly from me, the medical staff said. Tuberculosis was still raging in many parts of the world and being stuck in the DP camps with so many other migrants, who knew where the contagion came from.

I was abed for the whole first month in the hospital. I received daily doses of a number of shots and medicines. Some of these were to stop the blood hemorrhages and illness; some to fortify my weakened body. When I was finally allowed to get out of bed, my legs wobbled and I stumbled to stand. I needed to relearn to walk on my own. I was home for a couple of days and felt like a stranger as my family kept their distance and all I ate with was handled with extra care and washings. At age 12, I should have been sent to the children's sanitarium quite far from the city. Doctor Longtin felt compassion for the financial difficulty my parents were in: had I been so far, when would they be able to visit me? So together they agreed to register me as 14 years old so I could be placed at St. Joseph de Rosemont Sanitarium on the east end of the island. It was still far from where we lived but reachable by bus, and that was good for the family.

  Needless to say, I was the youngest patient there. My three roommates were 16-and- over French-Canadian girls. I don't recall how many patients the hospital housed, but in the five floors of many rooms, there was quite a diversity of women in our half of the building. The other half of the building housed the men. During the next 13 months, I received at first two X-rays a month, which eventually decreased to once a month, and weekly tests to confirm the presence of the tuberculosis bacteria. The weekly tests were done by extracting stomach fluids with a tube inserted through the throat, and when that became almost impossible for the gagging, it was slowly inserted via the nostrils. I can tell you it was horrible and often painful. My nose passages felt raw, and I am sure that was the beginning of my sinus problems which pop up sporadically to this day. I loathed those days when the doctor visits were due.

My youth and my background meant I was naive and innocent compared to the other girls, and the stories they regaled us with added much to my sexual education. Like when Fernande, a 17-year-old roommate from Montreal, managed to have secret meetings with a boy of the same age in the X-ray room and lab on a lower floor described to us their sexual escapades. However, they were discovered by the nuns and forbidden to meet. I also learned about the different people of Canada. Marthe was from the Maritime province of Prince Edward Island, situated far away near Nova Scotia on the Atlantic Coast, and told us about her way of life in a small fishing village. I do recall her telling us of some homes that were built partly inside of caves on the cliffs near the ocean. They were both fishermen and farmers. Her mother came once to see her in the 13 months we shared Room 315. Lorraine, a pretty 16-year-old from Pierrefonds just a little southwest of Montreal, was declared cured and left just after her 17th birthday in March 1956. On the same third floor, Therese, a beautiful girl about the age of my oldest sister, who was then in another hospital further away north of Montreal, and like her was engaged to be married, had an operation to remove a lung. But afterwards her fiancé deserted her. Therese was devastated and that contributed to her solemn view on life. The hardest part was when she asked us girls to her room to help her choose the dress she planned to be buried in. She was adamant it should have long sleeves to hide her bony arms. The operation had not succeeded in eliminating the illness and shortly after she passed away. We attended a mass in her memory in the hospital chapel and were thanked by her parents for the enduring kindness we had shown her. We all new that an early death could be our fate also if the treatments were not successful.

On a day like so many others a new patient arrived on a stretcher. Us curious girls stretched into the hallway not obeying the nurses to keep to our room. We believed we saw an elderly lady being brought into Therese's now empty room. Then the oxygen tent was brought up to the room. My friends and I thought she must also have been admitted for an operation. As the weeks went on, we were invited to say the rosary with the nuns in her bedroom. I remember a day when a handsome man of about 35 came with two toddlers to visit her, and to our amazement we learned she was only in her late 20s and these were her husband and children. Our prayers became more fervent then, until the final day when her widowed husband came to take her body away for burial. In later years I surmised the woman had not succumbed to TB but lung cancer. The thing that stayed with me was the recollection that, as sick as she was, she would beg to be let out of the oxygen tent so she could enjoy a smoke two or three times a day. . . maybe that is why I never took up smoking.

I saw my parents about once a month, and Bianca came once towards the end of my stay. Giuliana had been in and out of the other hospital. She was lucky that her fiancé was as much in love with her as ever and plans for their wedding progressed well. Because of her medical history, she was not allowed to enter my hospital, so I did not see her until I was allowed weekends at home in late June 1956.

Funny how some friends become closer to you and some instead keep a wider distance upon hearing of illness. Many of my parents' acquaintances kept their distance from the family—just the mention of TB brought fear among friends and neighbors. I had two good friends who stayed in touch with me, though, throughout this time. My old friend Mario from the German camp called me on the phone a number of times and sent me Italian books to pass the time with. I Tre Moschetieri (The Three Musketeers) and La Caverna dei Diamanti (The Diamond Mine) I read over and over. My fifth-grade Irish "boyfriend" Stanley sent me Treasure Island. I read continuously. These books are still part of my library.

Every two weeks we were entertained by good-willed artists who volunteered to perform for us. We gathered in the auditorium and saw dancers, heard singers, musicians and acts of different kinds. Otherwise we gathered in the auditorium to watch movies. The library on our floor carried magazines with articles of the actors and singers popular at the time. English and French singers came to entertain us. The

Chordettes' "Mr. Sandman"; Joan Weber's "Let Me Go, Lover"; "The Ballad of David Crockett" sung by Bill Hayes played on the radio, as well as Edith Piaf. Piaf sang not only of happy but also sad experiences and we related to those songs. I envied the dancer on roller skates who performed until his body was drained in sweat. I envied anyone who could do anything athletic without stopping every second for breath. Those were pleasant days and evenings. Often after supper we would gather in the solarium, and in the winter avidly watch the Canadians win their hockey games. Maurice Richard, Gordie Howe and Bobbi Orr were our favorite players.

Finally, in April 1956, I was allowed to go for a walk: first 15 minutes, then up to 30 minutes, every other, and then every day, around the neighborhood. It was about then also, I cannot recall the exact date, all the patients and staff gathered on the many terraces facing the main street to witness the change in the building's name from St. Joseph Sanitarium to St. Joseph Hospital. Tuberculosis was being conquered! The new medications, isoniazid and rifampin, were working well, and people by the hundreds were being cured of the scourge of TB. There was much jubilation then.

In late July I was dismissed by my doctor. I saw Dr. Longtin, whom I and my family admired, once a year for follow-ups. After three healthy years I was pronounced completely cured and safe from recurrence. Years later I learned the good doctor had died of the disease himself. He had saved my life, at the first hospital I had ever stayed in, and I think of and bless him for it even now.

V

While I was away, my family had moved from what was considered one of the poorest neighborhoods of the city to a much better side of town in a northern part of Montreal, with cleaner, newer row houses and a park nearby. In May 1957, Giuliana got married and moved not too far from us. Bianca worked in a clothes factory. Mamma, also, but soon she took in sewing at home, so she could be with me during the day. I helped her by turning the collars of the children's shirts she sewed right side out. Papà continued working for his Italo-Canadian employer and did well. In the fall, I was expected to return to school, sixth grade, but in a class I felt very old and out of place with the younger students there. Home schooling was granted; I studied and took some exams and was graduated to the Secondary Grade (high school). St. Pius X was a newer school on the northeast end of Montreal. I took the bus early every morning. School started before 8:30 a.m. and ended around 3:30 p.m. The classes were taught mostly by the Sisters of Saint Anne, a group of interesting Irish and some Scottish young, and not so young, women. It was an English school, but French was taught also, and Latin was still taught there. With my knowledge of Italian and previous experience with French, I managed to do very well all through the three years. I especially loved my literature classes—just loved Shakespeare, and Sir Walter Scott's poem "The Lay of the Last Minstrel," especially the sixth canto, is still a favorite of mine:

> Breathes there the man, with soul so dead,
> Who never to himself hath said,
> This is my own, my native land!
> Whose heart has ne'er within him burn'd. . . .

I have had occasion of borrowing those lines in my own writings many years later. It seemed he wrote those lines for me and all the immigrants on foreign soil. They are just as moving and relevant today as in his time. You travel to new places and establish new homes, new lives, but the place you were born never really leaves your heart.

The teen years are a time of bewilderment and confusion for most and for me that confusion was tripled. I had started those years away from the heart of my family and came home feeling a little strange and different. The experiences of the hospital left memories that lingered for years. When Giuliana came to visit and would talk about her newly married life with Mamma, I often giggled knowingly and was scolded for knowing too much. My mother was always reticent about sex. In our house, it was papà who was more open about sexuality and its education. But still, even he was very careful about what and how much was discussed. I was supposed to have been too young for such a subject.

The other thing that was difficult was watching my family, still a little uneasy with my healing, take the precaution of extra washing clothes and dishes I used every day—not until a couple of years later when Dr. Longtin made sure they understood the complete recovery I had undergone. I did not need to be kept at a distance from anyone anymore. I so needed to feel loved and wanted. I so missed being hugged. I had a whole year plus to make up for.

Fortunately friends who had stood by my side during the year in hospital continued to be there for me. Stan invited me to his home once. We talked and talked. I met his family, at least his siblings. His brother, who was a little older, gave me a brief hug and welcomed me. His sister accepted me without reservations and encouraged me to help her get supper ready. I learned how to make stuffed cabbage with her. The meal was delicious! Their mother was coming home late from work; I did not wait, wanting to get back home before dark. The friendship lasted a while, and then Stan and I went our different ways. He remains in my memory and heart, and I treasure always the gift of Treasure Island that brought me sunshine in those sad days in 1955. It holds a special place among the books on my shelves even now!

Mario was also still active in my life, but because his family lived on the west side of the city we did not see each other often. I was 16 and in the ninth grade (the last year of high school) and tired of being the oldest in the class. I missed having a real close friend. Mario was the one that called almost every day to see how I was coping, and I felt blessed for his friendship. One day we decided to get together on a school afternoon. Yes, I was naughty, and played hooky! We met at a park along the bus route to the west side of town. We saw a movie South Pacific at the Van Horne Theatre and then we went to his home in northwest Mont Royal. He played his guitar and sang a couple of songs for me. He sounded so much like Elvis Presley he could have doubled for him. After a while we took a walk across from the apartment house he lived in. On a tree there, there might still be an etched heart with our initials. The school called home to see if I was OK. The slap I received from my mother when I returned home had been well earned, but I did not regret the escapade. My face burned for a while that night and my ego was bruised, but the friendship lasted. No more secret meetings though. The lesson was learned! The funny part was that whenever he called me he would relate his experiences with the other girls he dated. We were like brother and sister and that was good for me. The friendship that lasted over seven years gave me some stability and assurance.

Slowly smiles returned and new friendships were formed. One of the French neighborhood boys asked me to go to a movie with him. I was thrilled! After the movie (I do not recall what we saw) we stopped in at his home for a soda and chips. His parents and sister left us alone in the parlor. It did not take me long to know that he wanted more than just time to watch a little TV and have a snack. My upbringing told me "No, no," and there the friendship ended.

Bianca was dating and some of our good Italian friends also, so I relented, and during the last year at St. Pius X, I became the "steady" of a Sicilian boy. The customs of those families were much stricter than those of my own family. For instance, girls needed to always be chaperoned and their parents' permission to date, but at our house we just needed to tell our parents with whom we were going and where and the expected time of our return home. We broke up, and two years later he was engaged to a beautiful girl from his region of Italy and hopefully had a wonderful marriage. The suspicious minds of his people would not permit our friendship to continue. His bride-to-be would never allow me to even attend their wedding, though I wished them the very best of futures.

I graduated high school with an average grade of 92% and was very proud, as were my parents. I so wanted to continue my studies. I excelled in science and wanted to become a pharmacist. But Papà said we could not afford more schooling. Giuliana had married and no longer contributed to the family income. I was needed to go to work and earn money to help with the family finances. Dad had finally bought a car, and he needed help to pay for the monthly premiums.

So at the ripe age of 17, I took secretarial courses and upon graduation in six months was employed at the firm of a group of notaries (equivalent of civil lawyers in the Napoleonic law practiced in Quebec, Canada). Starting as a receptionist, my knowledge of Italian, English and French gave me an edge, and I doubled as the office's translator. My earnings were nice, and I liked my co-workers and meeting all the people who came to the office in search of legal help.

Just about that time I started dating a young man about three years older than I. The love bug bit me and nothing else mattered!

My boyfriend was a jeweler by trade, a very good one. He also took acting classes at night and became the director of our small Italian theater group. We performed mainly in our parish hall. Our friends were a fine group of talented youngsters with love of theater and music in their hearts. English, Italian and some French songs were listened and danced to in our home basements—most homes had finished or semi-finished rooms in the basements—and at the Italian Soccer club to which most of us belonged. For my part our romance was going great, but after almost three years of dating, some hugging and kissing, a little necking was all that happened. The Italian girls and boys in our entourage were pairing off and finding fiancées and getting married. I love you was said, but no promise of more serious involvement.

Then during a long discussion I understood the why. His father's family had belonged to the aristocratic class back in Italy and even boasted of having a document from Napoleon Bonaparte, thanking them for the donation of land for his exploits. His mother was a maid in that household till she married one of the owner's sons. She wanted her boy to marry someone with a pedigree. She also expected to have a daughter-in-law who would serve her every wish as she had served before. My family, instead, was known for its independence, even us girls. My father's parents had been landowners also—my grandfather a horticulturist—but, no connection to Bonaparte or any other nobility. Our lineage came from hard-working folks who managed to live well—if not royally. In no way was I going to elope, as suggested, just so that his mother would be circumvented. Many years later on a visit to his mother, I learned that the other younger son had finally left the family and Montreal. He married a Hawaiian beauty of whom she did not approve. She was *different*.

VI

Another year passed and the friends around me were one after the other married. By this time, Bianca worked for an Italian builder. The Barone family lived on the east end of Montreal, in St. Leonard. A cousin of theirs came to visit from the United States. He and Bianca took a liking to each other and dated. Soon after, they decided to marry. Our family's one concern was that she would live in the US. New Jersey seemed very far, but my father's hopes of getting closer to his nephews now living in Kansas City, Missouri, made it seem a blessing. So in a few months Bianca was married in Montreal. I was one of her bridesmaids. The new couple moved to North Trenton, New Jersey. We were happy for her but sad at the thought she would be far from us; we promised to visit as often as we could.

I enjoyed my work with the law firm and grew to hold a place of respect within the Italian community. Many immigrants came to the office for their legal necessities, especially translation of documents for their legal immigration status, driver licenses and, of course, the often needed procura (power of attorney) to send back home to family. I was greeted and recognized in stores, at church, at parties and felt well appreciated.

Meanwhile two of the fellows in the office asked me on a date. The French Canadian notaire was a very intelligent fellow, but, really, I did not find him handsome enough to attract me in that way. But there was a handsome, young new notary who I liked a lot. When, after one year of working together, he finally asked me for a date, I agreed.

The intention was to go with another couple friends of his to a chalet in the Laurentians, a mountain range north of the city. He, of course, hinted, and I agreed, to perhaps pass the night there. I was tired of being branded the good girl—everyone's sister. So in my mind, this was the night I would give up my "Good-Girl" standing. The ride was easy and the view of the Laurentians stupendous. A lovely dinner at a nearby inn and then to the chalet for music and . . . almost . . . almost . . . but my heart was not in it. When the coddling got heavy, I realized, this is not what I want; I would only be giving in to peer pressure.

So my friends were all getting married, and those who were not attached no longer were held to the European norms their families raised them on. They became, as we said at the time, Canadians, a little looser in their morals. Perhaps wrongly, but at the time all the immigrants thought that the Canadians were loose and promiscuous. Talk about prejudice! For my part, I just could not do this to my family, I rationalized.

"Sorry, I'm just not ready for this. We would have tonight, and then you would go on to the next girl. Would you be very hurt if I asked you to bring me back home?"

A total gentleman, "I wish my sister might have your fortitude," he said.

So by two o'clock I was back home and in my own bed. We remained co-workers and even remained friends. I thank my luck to have known such a gentleman. It would be a lucky girl that became his wife.

VII

I was now 21 and still unattached. Had a few dates with some nice fellows but no one special. On December 28, 1964, two younger girlfriends called me, "Please, if you come with us our parents will surely let us go, please, please, come."

The soccer club to which all our families belonged to was having a New Year's Eve Dance. Their parents did not want to attend and would not let the girls go without an adult. Also, the club served alcohol and adult supervision was required. So to make the girls happy I capitulated and agreed to be their chaperon. It was the first time that I went out with an all-girls group. So far all my outings to such events had been with a male date.

The party was a success. We had a great time as we spent the hours towards 1965 in good company and much dancing. Two Italian young singers had been hired to keep the evening happy. I knew the fellows. One was a tenor named Mario (I have since forgotten his last name) who sang more of the classical songs. He was taking opera classes at the time. The tenor was rather short, a little on the heavy side, and also a Southerner. I danced with the other singer that night— also named Mario. He sang more pop songs in Italian, English and French. He had been dating one of the girls in our drama club for a while, and so I did not pay much attention to him at the time. But, as we danced, I realized how handsome he was. His black curly hair and those eyes so dark brown you seemed to be looking down a deep well—the charm just oozed from him. He escorted me, holding on to my elbow, back to my seat. His eyes lingered on me as he said, "Grazie, arrivederci?" (Thank you, see you again?) My knees felt weak and I hurriedly sat down.

On the way home my friends were grateful for my company and told me they also had made some promising contacts with one or two fellows. All I could think about was getting home and putting my feet up. I loved to dance, and once started did not like to sit any number out, especially since at the club we had some wonderful dancers, even a couple who actually were dance teachers. Most Saturday evenings, no matter how tired we girls were—even when we begged to get off doing some unfinished chores due to a headache or other reason—come seven o'clock the pretty dresses would come out and my blue dancing sandals were on my feet.

"Bello," Mamma or Papà would say, "Nice the headache is gone, right?"

They would accompany us to the club for they also had a good time with their friends there. Our club nights were family affairs, not like the night clubs of today. The young people would dance. The parents would pass the time reminiscing and singing many of the well-known Italian songs, while they played a round or two of cards . . . no betting, who had money to play with at that time? Good clean fun was had by all.

During the brief Canadian summers we took a couple of trips to the beach. The beach here consisted of a sandy spot in the Plage-Idéale on the riverbank of the Riviere de Prairie (River of the Prairies) north of Montreal. Often we would go with or meet up with a group of our Italian friends. A river is very different from the sea. Sea water is clear and the buoyancy of the salted water makes it easier to float and swim, and the sea floor is often sandy or rocky, whereas the river is mostly muddy and gooey. It is this muddy bottom that makes the water murky and keeps it from being clear.

In this very water, in that Plage-Idéale, we lost a dear friend. Angelo was a strapping, handsome, six-plus-feet tall 18-year-old when he accompanied his siblings to the beach one summer. He did not want to go, but on the insistence of his younger sister and brother, he drove them to the beach. Later that afternoon another friend called my father and we learned, with great sorrow, that our dear Angelo had apparently drowned in the river. The whole family gathered and met other friends there. It was difficult to console our young friends. The sister blamed herself for insisting he drive them. The brother, who was almost as tall as Angelo, could not swim and was unable to go to his aid. The lifeguards took too long to try and get to our friend. Two sunbathers at the beach were divers but only offered to help find his body for a fee after the fact. All night the men in our group, including my father, took turns in a police-provided canoe dredging the river. Not until near sunrise did they finally retrieve his corps in what was six feet two inches of water! His feet tangled in some vegetation at the bottom of the river. The coroner said he probably suffered a heart attack before drowning. Angelo had had a car accident a couple of days before that is why he had not wanted to drive all the way to Plage-Idéale.

All friends gathered around the grieving family. It was so sad to witness the first loss of someone we considered one of us in our new country. For me, this cemented the fear of swimming, especially of having my face under water. Even now when at a beach, I will only go swimming if a good swimmer is near me, and years went by before I could put my face under water either in the ocean or a swimming pool.

VIII

A week into 1965 my cousin called to ask me if he should give my phone number to a guy named Mario who was looking to contact me. I said of course he could. The Mario I assumed asking for a date was the tenor. He was the first who came to mind from the New Year's Eve party.

"Yes, you may pick me up for a movie on Saturday night," I had told him and waited for a chance to go on a good date.

During the week I often ate a quick lunch at an Italian restaurant near my workplace. "Bianca e Franco" was very popular because of the authentic dishes that were served there. Many Italians and others made it their favorite lunchtime place. Often we shared tables with friends and strangers due to its popularity and rather small available seating.

When Saturday finally came around, I was ready for my date with Mario. It was a very pleasant surprise when the ring of the doorbell brought me face-to-face with the handsome Mario with whom I had a dance on New Year's Eve—with whom I had on occasion, I realized, shared a table at "Bianca e Franco" our favorite lunch stop. The little flower bouquet he presented to my mother was an added attraction. Well done, what a smooth operator is what I thought at the moment. Could this get any better? Well, you can judge for yourself.

We got to his car, a green Fiat 600, and he immediately opened the front passenger door. "Oh, what a gentleman!" I thought. To my astonishment he quietly added, "Sorry, please, I must go in first. You see the driver side door is broken. It will not open".

Do I go back to my apartment and leave him there—quickly, it's your decision to make! But what the heck, he is so handsome, those curls and those well-deep brown eyes.

"OK, Mario, will the car bring us to where we are going?"

He tells me not to worry and thanks me for letting him in first. He gives the key a turn and we are off. In this cold, January, Canadian winter night we are headed for one of the few Italian-movie-showing theaters in our city. I felt a strange premonition as he explained we were going to see one of the latest Marcello Mastroianni's films Divorzio all'Italiana (Divorce Italian Style). What kind of omen was that? What will this date amount to?

From that day on I saw him every day. He would meet me as I left the office every afternoon and drive me home. Often he would stay for supper, at my mother's invitation. He would always have some small, but appropriate, gift for mamma. It took Mario a whole two weeks before he asked me to marry him. When I asked my mother what she thought of him she said, "He is either a very good catch, or too good to be true. Be careful."

When I told my boss that I was engaged to be married, he took me into his office, sat me down in front of him and told me he wanted me to have two things: he would prepare a pre-nuptial agreement and I was to insist on a life insurance policy signed and delivered before the wedding.

"Should he decide to break the engagement you have the necessary weapons to sue him with."

We met with Padre Pini, a parish priest and friend. He was stunned by the news we gave him as we asked if he would officiate. Taking me aside he warned me, "Do you know this guy? Only a few months ago I was told he was to marry so-and-so, and before that another woman said she wanted to marry him. Are you sure he is honest with you?"

I knew both the girls in question but knew that to be wishful thinking on their part. Mario sang in clubs throughout the city and had even recorded a 45 record. He was known in the Italian and French press. About two months into the engagement he won a prize for his singing. The French reporter asked him what the future would bring, and he said marriage to . . . and introduced me as his fiancée. I got the coldest stare from that young girl. Nothing was ever published about his winning in her paper. The Italian paper ran a story saying that the young singer had won and "of course, his name is always attached to Moira's"—another Italian female singer whom he had dated for a time. That was in the past before we began to date. They would soon enough know about our relationship.

The priest then called my fiancé into his office. I was told that he warned him against hurting me for according to him I was a very good girl and was to be treated with the highest respect. We left the office with his blessings. Mario and I laughed as we shared each other's conversations with our friend and promised each other we indeed would love only each other from that day on.

As was the custom in Italy, my mother and sister Giuliana went to work on my trousseau, as well as the clothes for my wedding and honeymoon. Giuliana had learned much about clothing designs, preparations and sewing at the liceo in Italy. She had the uncanny talent of looking at a dress and repeating the style on her own without using a pattern. My wedding dress was copied from a European princess' wedding whose picture had been in the Italian newspaper. A simple A-line, three-quarter-sleeve dress in a smooth peau de soie (skin of silk) fabric just at shoe length. The veil that I put on my head was made with three plies of tulle: a sturdy layer on the underpart of the veil for the pouf effect, another for the relaxed flow, and the top tier, which took about two months to finish, had a honeycomb effect with the tulle gathered and sewn into little squares, held by small ribbon bows and each white satin bow was attached with two seed pearls in the center. This gave a honeycomb effect to the whole veil. The veil was long and went way past my feet when kneeling. A few things for my future home were gathered. The one set of bed linens I was embroidering, never quite completed. I did not have time to finish the pillowcases. Oh well, it would be easier to purchase these items once we had our own home.

  I had found my prince or rather he found me. Together we planned our simply beautiful wedding. We found we could afford about 180 guests. The list made, we proceeded to write the invites in both English and Italian. Together we delivered the invitations to family and friends. Yes, actually hand delivered them, since the

Poste Canadiennes (Canadian Postal Service) were on strike the two months before our chosen date.

We signed the pre-nupt our notary prepared for us, and five days before the wedding we invited an insurance agent friend to my parents' apartment to write the life insurance my boss had required. We passed a couple of hours talking. As good Italian hosts we offered some appetizers and passed the wine bottle around in celebration. Mario and the agent had a little more wine than needed. I still wonder how our friend made his late night drive home safely. Mario was in no condition to drive, so I insisted he stay the night. Soon, after my parents went to bed, we spent the rest of the night together on the floor on a make-shift mattress in my living room. My heart was pumping wildly as I climbed under the covers with him. Our kisses became more and more demanding. Hands traveled as we explored each other's bodies. I had not drunk so much but still felt tipsy at the excitement of it all. I lost my virginity that night and learned how wonderful sex shared with the one you love can be.

We wed on beautiful September 6, 1965 (Labor Day) in the Italian parish church where I had received my Confirmation. Padre Pini officiated at the wedding and gave us his personal blessing. The smile on my face in the wedding pictures tells it all.

Among the guests were my cousins and their wives from Missouri. It had taken 15 years, but for the first time since leaving Lesum, Germany, we were reunited. They had come to Montreal just on the special occasion of the youngest of cousin's wedding day. I felt very special to be so honored, though a little sad. Bianca had married a US citizen and was waiting for her green card at that time. The authorities warned her she may not be able to return to New Jersey if she left the country. So, afraid, she was not able to attend her younger sister's wedding. I missed her being there. Mario had a brother and sister-in-law and friends as guests, and we had a lot of friends in common who came to celebrate with us.

IX

We had both decided that we could borrow some extra money and either buy a large engagement ring or take a long honeymoon. I never really cared about jewelry, so it was a no-brainer. We would go to Italy, so I could meet the rest of Mario's family. We left all our guests at the reception as soon as the repast was ended and we had taken our first dance together. We had hired a friend of ours and his band, and as he sang "Love is a Many Splendor Thing" we held each other close, kissed and then waved good-by to all. We hurriedly changed into traveling clothes, and by 6:00 p.m. we boarded the TWA plane for Frankfurt, Germany, the first stop on our honeymoon. Our wedding night was spent playing card games over the Atlantic and wishing and anticipating what was to come.

On arriving in Frankfurt we made our way from the Central Station to the hotel. We found that the hotel we thought had our reservation had no record of it. We found another hotel near the train station and a comfortable room. Do you know that German beds are soft and have feather mattresses and quilts? At least ours had. We were excited to experience our first night together as husband and wife and our first legal sexual union at ease with no worry of who else was near. The desire grew rapidly and our love was leading us to the heavenly promise. Gosh, try as we might, the mattress did not allow for proper alignment of our bodies. The center of the mattress just fell in, enveloping our two bodies in a tight bun. There was no way to consummate our marriage in that feather bed! In frustration and anticipation we laid our feathery quilt on the floor and then, oh yes, then heaven was mine!

The rain in Spain may stay on the plain, but it was never-ending gray days in Frankfurt and would be in Paris, France, which was supposed to be our next stop. According to the weather predictions, it would rain for most of the rest of September. I drooled at each shop window that had sausages hanging from the ceiling and sauerkraut in the barrels. Mario is not a lover of foreign cuisine, so I found out. All he looked for was a proper place to eat in, which to him meant Italian food. So for the next couple of days, I tasted some wonderful street food, while he enjoyed at least a pint or two of great German beer, but we dined at the newly found "Mario Ristorante Italiano."

We did not want to be gloomy for long, so we decided to at least be with family in a gayer place, so on to Italy. At Rovello Porro near Lake Como, where my sister-in-law lived, I found a very comfortable home and lovely people in my sister-in-law, her husband and children, and the friendly neighbors there.

We had time to visit Milano, a mere 19 miles south, a big commercial city with large shopping malls known for its fashion industry. We visited the famous the Duomo di Milano (Cathedral of Milan). The Duomo looks like lace work with its ornate delicate-looking gothic architectural style. From the roof there is a beautiful view of the whole city. At the top spire of the Duomo stands the famous statue La Madonnina, a statue of St. Mary that was placed there in 1774 and is the patroness of the Milanesi (people of Milan). Some of the museums we wished to visit were closed, as was the opera house, La Scala, undergoing off-season repairs. On the way out of Milan, the train passed the station of Saronno, and the fresh aroma of the Amaretti di Saronno (almond cookies and liquors loved all over the world) permeated the area for miles. We visited Como and the site of Alessandro Volta's laboratory and his birthplace in 1745, inventor of the first electric battery and who gave the name of volt to power of electricity. We toured the lago (lake) and the beautiful mountains that surround the area and hint at the

Italian-Swiss Alps just beyond. A few days more in the lovely northern town then south to Mario's hometown in the province of Campobasso. There I was welcomed and doted over and totally spoiled by my father-, sisters-, brothers-, niece- and nephews-in-law. That loan was well spent indeed!

Then another visit north to my area of Italy. We took the train to Padova for a visit to St. Antonio's Basilica. St. Anthony of Padua is venerated all over the world by Italian immigrants and their families. We rented a car and drove to Trieste. The city of my childhood had grown into a busier place than I remembered. My cousins greeted us and showed us around. Unlike my in-laws that offered up their own bedrooms and did not want us to rent rooms elsewhere, my cousins' first question was, "Where are you staying?" No hint of invitation to stay at their apartments. They were all well-off and did share their good fortune by taking us to the best restaurants in town and showering us with wedding gifts. We took the ferry to Capodistria, my sometimes childhood home; my uncle, who now lived in Trieste, wanted to show me were the apartment I had lived as a young child was.

"No need," I told him. From the port where the ferry had dropped us off, I walked him to Nonna Piccia's house located on via Porta Grande then to the Piazza della Fontana, so named for the big fountain in its center, which I had played in as a child, and on to the flour mill and the apartment above it where I once lived. The people who lived there now were Slavs and did not understand me when I told them in Italian that I had lived there a few years at the end of the war. I was not invited to enter the lodging but was politely told, "Adios." From there I walked the street that led to the kindergarten and elementary school Bianca and I had attended as children.

The singing housewives I remembered, the open windows, the children playing in the streets and piazzas were gone. Houses all had closed windows and shutters, and as we approached an opened doorway, someone would bolt inside and close up before we could reach them. It was a sad city with sad, empty streets. I felt a deep sense of loss and longing for the old happy days of my childhood. Then we visited the cemetery where my grandparents had been laid to rest, and I spent a little time with my godmother/aunt and the two uncles who had remained behind for different reasons. My nonni were already in their 80s when we left and did not want to leave their home, their farm and their children. My zio Francesco had been crippled with polio in his childhood; his arms and legs were affected, yet he managed to do some wonderful work as a shoemaker. Friends had duped him into signing up with the communist party in the 1920s thus would not have been allowed to emigrate. His brother, Guerino, was feebleminded and never quite developed to an adult mental age, and so he too was no candidate for migration. My aunt and godmother, Elisabetta, did not want to leave them alone, since at a young age she had devoted herself to helping her parents care for the home and her siblings. They lived and died in their parents' home.

At my nonna's house, I looked right away for the large scale they used to weigh the vegetables they sold and which I played with every time I visited. The scale was always kept in the attic in the cubbyhole above the stairs one took to reach the attic storage. To my chagrin it was gone! My zia said they had sold it to a neighbor not long before my arrival. The one other thing I wanted they freely gave me. It was a wall clock that hung on their kitchen wall. I packed it carefully for the trip back to Canada.

With a girl cousin we went to beautiful Venice, but the visit there was too short. San Marco Square with the legions of pigeons—I have a nice picture of one eating from my hand—the many bridges we saw and stores we visited were great. The restaurant with its fresh seafood from the area was a real treat. We met my cousin-in-law who had just come into port; he was the chef on an ocean liner. Other cousins were also on ships: one as an ocean liner captain and one as a chief mechanic in the boiler room. We spent a little time with them over a dinner or two back in Trieste. There we visited the beautiful Castello di Miramar built by Archduke Fernand Maximilian of Hapsburg. It was to be his and his wife's, Charlotte of Belgium, residence. It is built right on a cliff above the sea and is surrounded by a beautiful park with many splendid plants from different parts of the world. An old family story says that my great-grandfather was on security duty as a soldier on one of the owner's visits, and Charlotte lost her engagement ring in the sea below. He dove in immediately and retrieved the ring. The Archduke wanted to thank him, "Anything you want." The humble man just asked for an office job rather than active fighting duty. He spent the rest of his military service sitting behind a huge desk . . . so we were told by the family.

On again southward back to Mario's hometown. From there, our next side trip was to be Roma. The night before our visit to the capital Mario ate one of his favorite dishes, sautéed hot peppers. He and his siblings ate to their fill. They paid for it dearly the next day while walking all around Rome. We visited the Vatican - St Peters and the Sistine Chapel; he suffered, I giggled, especially when I insisted on visiting every room in the Castel Sant' Angelo on the east side of the Tevere (Tiber) River. We found a lovely pensione (inn) for the night and had a good rest. Next day we were in Naples, where we had the most wonderful chioppino (fresh fish stew) in a family friend's trattoria. On the visit to Pompeii my husband said I took movies of every rock there; he had a hard time making me keep up with him. We were following a guided tour group, but I wanted to delve more into each site we saw, from the copies of petrified bodies caught by the Mount Vesuvius's eruption to the wall frescoes and the statues and fountains in the Roman gardens. You even see how they used the public restrooms and the numerous whore houses with the suggestive wall décor. One of the better preserved Vettii's villa boasts a fresco in its entrance of a male figure with a very well-endowed penis. It was explained that we saw many such pictures in the homes since the picture represented the wishes for good fortune and fertility for the family who lived there (not unlike the horn used as good luck charm by the people from Sicily).

    The Amalfi Coast came next with its tight turns on a road high up the sheer cliffs that jut onto the Mediterranean Sea. We stopped in Amalfi, Sorrento and other small towns. The vistas, the food, the people — all one of a kind and the most welcoming of hosts. To get to Capri, we took a speedboat that barely skims the water and seems to fly across the sea. The funiculare, a bus that travels on rails and is powered via an electric cable, brings you up the high slopes of the island. Oh, yes! Capri, at a restaurant on a balcony with a gorgeous view of the sea, two little imps stood by the door not only panhandling but sort of sizing up the customers. My husband had warned me not to speak to them for he spoke the local dialect; he'll do all the talking. But I was caught off guard and turned to them and asked in proper Italian what they wanted. They both ran inside the restaurant and yelled.

    "O Dio (God)! He is Napoletano and she is a Italiana!" (He's from Naples and she is a foreigner.)

    I told the owner that I was Italian. We had a good laugh and a wonderful lunch — again the freshest of fish. For the rest of our honeymoon I was mainly known by the residents of that south-central part of Italy as la forestiera (foreigner).

Our three-month-long honeymoon came to an end all too soon. Time came to fly back to Montreal. It was difficult for me to think of Canada as my home, when I felt so at home right there in that small town in the Matese mountains. In December we packed our gifts, including a chandelier and some cheese. Dry sausages and other goodies, even though we told them some things were not allowed, made it into our luggage. With our hearts full of both love and heartache — Mario especially felt the sadness: he was leaving his hometown again, his aging father, his sisters, brothers-in-law, and nephews and nieces. On the way to Rome to catch our plane, we again stopped by the cemetery to say a prayer at Mario's mother's and sister-in-law's tombs. He had been in Montreal when his mother died in 1962 and that ache was fresh in his heart now.

The flight back was uneventful. We sat holding hands, each knowing what the other was thinking. Our kisses told of how we felt, of the ache at the departure, as well as the excitement and hope for our future life together.

After we landed, the customs person asked us if we carried more than we went with. By the Italian name on his badge, I felt sure he would understand.

"We were on our honeymoon and visited with the family we left behind many years ago. Everyone gave us wedding presents. You name it, it's there," and I pointed to the over-bulging suitcases and extra boxes that had cost us $100.00 for the extra weight. He laughed and checked just the one bag we had as carry-on. In it he found a roasted, stuffed squab my sister-in-law had hidden even after we insisted we could not take it with us. "You keep that," I told him, "Enjoy."

He smiled and whispered, "Grazie!"

Three unforgettable months—among the precious memories especially—the love by and for my new expanded family. Who knows, with God's help, one of these days we will make it to Paris to continue our honeymoon.

X

Back in Montreal we still lived with my parents. How do you terrify a newlywed? Just have her brand-new husband get sick and need an ambulance trip to the hospital. Mario's kidney stones caused him much pain, and I cried and held his hand all the way to the hospital. Mother Nature took care of the stones with a little help from our doctor and lots of lemonade (the acidity of the lemons breaks up the calcium-formed stones). After a couple of days, he was well enough to return home.

My mother reminded me of our talk before the wedding. I had asked her, "How do you know if the person you love is really the right one for you?" She told me to consider two things:

"If that person gets very sick, would you be willing to help him take care of his basic needs? Yes, even help him wipe after a toilet run. And secondly, would you still stay with him if he proved to be infertile and unable to give you the children I know you want?"

I had pondered all that and prayed for guidance, and after this ordeal I knew I had chosen well. This man would be "my man" for life and evermore.

We moved to a larger apartment in a newer neighborhood. On the way following the movers, our car, the Fiat 600, gave up its soul. With fond memories we let it go to the junk yard. I proved to be pregnant as well—that last night in Italy had done the trick. We were very happy and waited anxiously for the arrival of our first child. I attended Lamaze classes and was ready to have a natural birthing experience. Month after month that summer, as I showed more and more, I was proudly walking as if on clouds, happy as could be. Then as September approached and I knew I reached and passed the time I was supposed to deliver, I got anxious. Finally, my doctor said he believed I was now a full month overdue and we needed to be prepared to induce the birth. There went my hopes for a nice, natural birth. Mario was more upset then I was; he had lost a sister-in-law at childbirth and any hint of a problem scared him.

The birth was induced on September 10, 1965. I was admitted at 6:00 a.m. and at seven received the first injection to help with the inducement. This method is difficult to undergo: the non-existent labor pains manifest themselves immediately at a strong pitch. The nurses were constantly checking on me, but I wasn't the only patient. Unfortunately, there was another mother expecting the birth of a very large child—turned out to be a boy of 11 pounds—while she was a small woman under five feet tall. We both shared the same doctor, Dr. Morrie Gelfand. I had often seen her during my monthly visits to his office. So we were both there at Jewish General Hospital at the same time, both having difficult deliveries. When Dr. Gelfand checked me I was only a little dilated and dry, no liquid followed as he stripped the membrane of the uterus. Apparently my waters had dripped slowly over time without my noticing. The birth would be difficult, but it must happen now for the baby did not have the protection of the amniotic fluid in the uterus. Despite the urgency, the labor pains were not at their peak, and the hours passed from morning to noon to late afternoon. I stopped being nice and calm and started to cry and scream. Mario was pacing the floor and had a hard time hiding the tears in his eyes when I grasped his hand for courage. Later I heard from his brother just how scared he had been and how he cried for me and how many cigarettes he had consumed in the lobby.

By 6:00 p.m. all I kept saying was, "Take this baby from me. Give me a Cesarean. I need the pains to stop." I was exhausted from the heavy and frequent labor pains. The doctor, in his white coat, traveled from my room to the other woman's room, until finally I heard the other baby's cries across the hallway. I was jealous, just wished it was mine! At 7:30 p.m. I finally gave birth to my first child. I know I looked at my daughter but was too exhausted to do anything but fall asleep. Mario kissed me and said how lovely our daughter was . . . he was crying tears of happiness now.

Later, back in my regular room, I was awakened by more strong pains. When I called for the nurse, she told me they were normal pains and was a little abrupt with me. I am sure they were all tired of hearing me cry all that afternoon. Finally, I told Mario to get the nurse. I could not ignore that the pains were as bad as the labor had been. She marched in to my bedside, apparently annoyed I had interrupted whatever was doing at the nurse's station, and felt my still large tummy. As she pressed, a little blood splattered all the way to the wall across the end of the bed. She gasped and Mario yelled, "O Dio!" I was hemorrhaging! I started sobbing. Immediately two other nurses jumped into the room—she must have summoned help—soon followed by my doctor. Mario was sent to the waiting room. I was rushed back to the delivery room. I noticed my doctor was wearing a tuxedo. It was five days before the Jewish New Year and the newly graduated doctors were to be presented with their diplomas that very night by my doctor, hence the tuxedo. He called for help, but all the anesthesiologist had left for the party. Dr. Goldsmith did not wait for anyone else. He apologize as he administered the anesthetic mask—the gas entered full force into my nostrils and lungs—I was out in a minute. While I slept he saved my life. I woke up later with Mario by my side. He was sweating with fear and relief that I and the baby had lived through the ordeal. We both cried and hugged and kissed.

Next day the nurse brought my daughter, Donatella, her face looked like the face of a month old child, not as she had looked the night before when just out of a mother's womb. I looked her over as the nurse undid her little blanket and explained that the wrinkles and what looked like scratches on her legs, feet, little arms and body were the result of the dry environment she had spent a few weeks in my uterus. She would heal fine and was anxious to be held by her mother. I felt her in my arms and cuddled her for a few minutes, kissed her and then begged the nurse to bring her back to the nursery for I needed to sleep some more. When visiting hours came and Mario and my mother entered the room, they were surprised not to see the baby there with me. Most new mothers had the bassinets left in their rooms during the day. I explained how tired I had been as I woke up. Unfortunately, due to my bout with Tuberculosis, I was encouraged not to breast feed. So all my children were to be bottle fed. But I loved them anyway and I think they knew it. To this day they are very close to me still. About a year later when I brought Donatella for a well visit, the pediatrician checked my record and said, "You were lucky. Had you been in any other hospital and with any other doctor, your daughter would be an orphan now."

Years later, complaining of problems with my sinuses, another doctor said I might sue the obstetrician for not waiting for the proper anesthesiologist. My reply, "I thank God and bless him always for saving my life and my daughter's mother on that night." How could people think of suing someone who gave them a chance to live?

And so we became a lovely young family. I had the help of my mother during the day; at night I was on duty with my new baby. I loved that time with her alone as we became acquainted with each other.

1. Gisella Steffè, mamma, circa 1940, Italia.

2. Giovanni Steffè, papà, circa 1940, Italia.

3. Nonna Piccia, Giovanna Starz Steffè, maternal nonna, circa 1940, Italia.

4. *Nonno Natale Steffe, maternal nonno, circa 1940, Capodistria.*

5. Nonna Grande, Margherita Zucca Steffè, circa 1946. Not pictured her husband Antonio Steffè. Pola, Trieste.

6. My eldest sister, Giuliana, at 6 years old. Pola, Trieste, 1941.

7. From left to right, brothers and sister Zio Guerino, Zia Elisabetta and Francesco Steffè on their way to the farm in Semedela. Capodistria, date unknown.

8. That's me on the left standing with my kindergarten friend Brunetta, circa 1946, Capodistria.

9. School Picture, circa 1946, Capodistria, Italia. Circled, left to right, me and my sister Bianca.

10. A postcard of the SS Skaubryn, circa 1950.

11. Left to right, me, Bianca, mom, and Giuliana sitting on the ground at the Gatekeeper' house on Montebello, Canada, 1952.

12. Side gate serving as our entrance to the estate. Montebello, Canada, 1952.

13. Left to right (back row) Mamma, Giuliana, papà. (front row) me and Bianca Steffè. Montebello, Canada, 1952.

14. My sister Bianca and I with our dog Diana looking for gold in the creek. Montebello, Canada, 1952.

15. My first communion. Posing next to the car my dad drove as a chauffeur. Montebello, Canada, 1952.

16. Mr. Cassidy's 4*th* Grade. A-Stanley, my first 'boyfriend', B-Bianca, C-Giamina, later my cousin Frank's first wife, D-me. Montreal, Canada, 1955.

17. St. Joseph of Rosemont Sanitarium, then Hospital. Rosemont, Montreal, Canada, 1955.

18. Patients giving a show. Rosemont, Montreal, Canada, 1955.

19. Papà's 48th birthday celebrated in our apartment. Montreal, Canada, 1959.

20. Giuliana and Angelo's engagement party. Montreal, Canada, 1956.

21. Giuliana and Angelo Pivetta's wedding day. Montreal, Canada, 1957.

22. With friends participating in a soap opera aired on the Italian Radio station. Montreal, Canada, 1964.

23. Appearing in one of the Italian Club's performances. Montreal, Canada, 1964.

24. Enjoying a day at the Plage-Ideale. Montreal, Canada, 1960.

25. Standing with my friend Angelo. Montreal, Canada, 1960.

26. Left to right, Frank, Giannina with baby Linda, me, papà, mamma, Bianca, Fred, Giuliana, Angelo, and Antonella aged 20 months. Montreal, Canada, 1963.

27. My first trip to Princeton, New Jersey, to visit Bianca and Fred. United States, 1964.

28. Mario Della Penta. Montreal, Canada, 1962 or 1963.

29. Mario Della Penta publicity photograph. Montreal, Canada, 1962.

30. *Our wedding day. Montreal, Canada, 1965.*

31. Mario and I in Piazza San Marco with Elisabetta Guirini, my cousin's daughter. Venezia, Italia, 1965.

32. The home where Nonna Piccia once lived. Capodistria, 1965.

33. Venetian architecture in Capodistria. 1965.

34. My parents-in-law Serafina and Donato Della Penta. Campochiaro, Italia, circa 1950.

35. My brothers-in-law Antonio Della Penta and Pasquale Iannarella (sitting) relaxing in the doorway of Mario's family home. Campochiaro, Italia, 1965.

36. Mario Della Penta with his father Donato Della Penta. Campochiaro, Italia, 1965.

37. Farm houses and barns in lower Campochiaro. Italia, 1965.

38. The Tower, a landmark in Campochiaro, sits at the top of the mountain overlooking the town. Italia, 1965.

39. Ruins in Pompeii. Italia, 1965.

40. Vic Vannelli, Sabrina's godfather, in front of Gentleman's Choice. East Brunswick, New Jersey, United States, 1970.

41. Advertisement for our grand opening. 1969.

42. Donatella and friend on the SS Sepia during our trip to Italia in 1971.

43. Our first house in East Brunswick. New Jersey, United States, 1972.

44. My daughters Sabrina (left) and Donatella (right) posing with Blaze. East Brunswick, New Jersey, United States, 1974.

45. From left to right, Giuliana, her daughter Antonella (holding Sabrina), her son Pier Paolo, Donatella and Angelo. Montreal, Canada, 1973.

46. Donatella and Sabrina playing with Bianca's daughters, Sandra (left top), Marisa (right top), Lisa (right bottom) and Claudia) left bottom). Hopewell, New Jersey, United States, 1975.

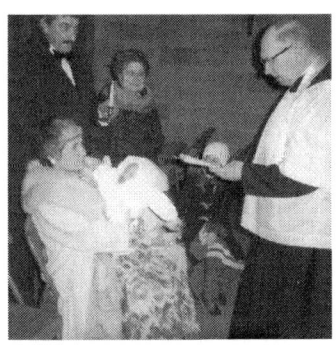

47. Daniela's christening. Her godparent's Pietro and Filomena Colacci. Princeton, New Jersey, United States, 1973.

48. Giuliana, Bianca and me. Long Beach Island, New Jersey, United States, 1973

49. Captain's Night on our cruise. 1976

50. Ghirardelli Square. San Francisco, California, United States, 1978.

51. Chilly boat ride to Alcatraz. San Francisco, California, United States, 1978.

52. Santa Barbara, California, United States, 1980.

Book Three—The United States

I

Autumn in Montreal is beautiful: the leaves on its many maple trees put on their many shades of yellow, orange, bright red, and as they fall to the ground, become a multi-colored carpet underfoot. I always loved the crinkly, scrounging sound under your feet and would walk rather than take the bus anywhere I could at that time. But autumn is short lived and in November the snow starts to fall. From then until late April, early May, winter weather is king. It can get down to 10 and even more below 0 Fahrenheit degrees on the coldest days. We who lived there for a few years had become rather accustomed to the weather. We took our sleds to the parks; we ice skated at the many rinks in the city; we built snow castles and had snowball fights with our friends.

Mario, however, showed signs of really suffering the cold Canadian winter. More and more he talked about finding somewhere warmer for us to live. My sister, now married to a US citizen, lived in New Jersey was happy there. The climate was much better, including warmer winters, with very little snow compared to Canadian winters. Slowly we planned and got ready for our first big move. Mario luckily, in early 1967, obtained a worker's visa with a business in Princeton, a hair shop owned by Italian immigrants right on Witherspoon Street, not far from the beautiful Princeton University campus on Nassau Street.

We had visited the town both before and after my sister's wedding and liked the cozy feeling of that area. My sister encouraged us—she and her husband would be happy to have us stay with them until Mario was settled with work and we could be on our own. It would mean leaving my parents and older sister and her family. Mario would be far from his brother and his family and his close friends in the city. Not an easy decision to make; we prayed and thought about it a lot. Talking it over with the families, they neither encouraged nor discouraged us. They had left their families much further, in Italy, in order to find a better life. Mario and I and our daughter were now our own family—we must think of what will be best for us. Our daughter and I would be in safe company with my parents for a bit, while he prepared a new life in the US. With a little anguish and a little excitement, within the year baby and I joined him in New Jersey.

II

Our relatives were glad to help us and for a while we shared their home. After a few months we moved into a nice apartment, part of a larger home in Princeton, owned by Italian-Americans. The lower part of their large home, which had served as den and playrooms for their growing boys who were now married and on their own, was easily made into a separate apartment big enough for the three of us. The property cornered Lawrenceville Road (Route 206) and Province Line Road, a more rural area of Princeton. There were no sidewalks but ditches on the side for the rain to gather. Next to the acreage with the triple barn and the many trees was a nursery business, which we liked. A little further up from us towards the town proper was the property of J. Seward Johnson, Sr., owner of Johnson & Johnson Co., and his once Polish maid, now third wife, Barbara Piasecka. The 140-acres estate was named Jasna Polana, bright glade, which Mrs. Johnson turned into a country club after her husband's death. On the southern corner of Lawrenceville and Province Line roads, Bristol-Myers Squibb built a huge company headquarter. On our side of Lawrenceville Road across from Province Line Road, a 10-foot fence hid property there from view . . . never did know who owned and lived there. From the property we lived on down to the Millstone River was all open land, used mainly for sod cultivation for years after we left the area. This rural area was much different from the urban life I was used to in Canada.

    Mario loved being with Italian people who shared much in common with him, especially when it came to food and drink. We made our own wine and shared their cold basement with them for our cask of the best white wine ever and hung our sausages and prosciutto to dry there. For a while life was good.

Mario and I were very much in love, and even though I was a bit afraid of trying, I did get pregnant again. But that second pregnancy was aborted naturally after just about four weeks. I told Mario that if I waited too long to get pregnant again I may never try, so here we went for the third time. This pregnancy was easy, and in February 1970 I was admitted in labor to the Princeton Hospital, again hoping for a nice, natural birth. Unfortunately, again nature took a detour; my second daughter was a breach birth. Baby decided she wanted to come out butt first. The obstetrician tried to turn the head towards the birth canal in vain. So this birth took a little longer than even the doctor wanted, but my second daughter was another beautiful girl. Her big sister was amazed and happy to see her. Again, as our family got larger, we were happy and terribly in love, but the sun was not always shining.

III

As nice as the area in Princeton was, I was very often lonely and depressed. In Montreal I worked and moved around independently. I had a social life with family and friends that I enjoyed. I always loved the open air and freedom of movement and independence instilled in me by my parents and continued within my marriage.

Mario used our one car to commute to work into town. In Canada, buses could be ridden very easily, as they stopped at their designated places about every 5-10 minutes. Here in Princeton, the buses came by our neighborhood every hour or so during rush hour and not on very reliable schedule. With a toddler and a newborn, it was difficult for me to go very far from home. Our apartment on ground level, surrounded by large, mature trees and bushes let very little light in through the windows. At times, with what my mind knew, but my heart did not fully accept, as postpartum depression, I felt like a prisoner and was afraid of falling further into a serious depression.

The apartment had some other issues also. The septic tank had not been properly maintained. Too many times the sewer would back up into our bathroom shower and sink, the sink is where I bathed our new daughter. We had no bathtub and even the young toddler had to take showers. I kept telling Mario we needed to move. I knew he liked our landlords for their background was not unlike his, but I needed more. I wanted a place where the sewer contents stayed where they belonged; where I did not have to tackle the dirty job of cleaning the sink and disinfecting it every time I wanted to use it; I needed light from windows above ground level. In Montreal I could be independently social. I worked and traveled around the city on my own. I needed to be with people and hear activity around me. Mario just did not understand my needs. We argued without fighting outright. But I kept warning him that I could not tolerate this for much longer and keep my sanity.

One day, after another sewer attack, he came home to find the apartment empty. With my sister and brother-in-law's help I moved back into their house. They had purchased a second home in Ewing, and their first house in North Trenton was up for rent. So I moved myself in. I think that opened Mario's eyes. He joined me, even if a little unhappy at first. I loved to walk with my daughters and meet neighbors and see life. The home was comfortable. We bought some furniture and proudly invited our friends over. I walked every day, weather permitting, with the toddler in tow and the baby in her carriage. The neighbors were friendly and caring. We spent some good months there. The home on Weber Avenue was close to Prospect Street, which led to North Olden Avenue, a busy commercial area with shops, department stores— Corvettes at that time—and the Trenton Farmers Market (still there today) that my sister and I would visit almost every Saturday for fresh vegetables and lots of Italian goods.

In time Mario was encouraged to open his own salon. A friend and client lived in East Brunswick, about 40 minutes away from us, and thought that it would be a great place for his business: East Brunswick was called the bedroom suburb of New York. People lived there, but many worked in New York City. With good traveling roads and buses and trains, it was easy to do the 30-odd miles into the Big Apple. People familiar with New York were thought to be more stylish, more in tune with international (European) fashion. All reasons Mario liked.

In December 1969 he opened his business with his friend as silent partner. His men's hairstylist shop became THE place for businessmen, professionals and young men of style. Doctors, attorneys, professors, both local and from as large an area as Philadelphia and professionals who worked in New York, became regulars and, with time, good friends. He was named more than once in the local and area-wide newspapers as the business to frequent. The only drawback was the distance from our home to the salon, especially in the dark winter evenings when the shop was opened until as late as nine o'clock and he would make it home only after ten.

At that time there was a city ordinance that mandated the unions to close certain businesses, like beauty salons, each and every Wednesday. It was also the habit for doctors and other professionals not to practice in their personal offices on those same days. Mario's clientele consisted of many of these professionals who took Wednesdays as their day off. After their early rounds of golf, they came to the salon to take care of their personal grooming needs. The Barber Union complained and started to harass our business and employees. They tried in every way to intimidate Mario into obeying their Union rules. Rudely, Union members even came to the shop smoking and dropping their cigar and cigarette ashes on our clean floors. Mario offered to teach them the specialty of hairstyling, rather than just the barbering the US schools then taught, to no avail. They said they would picket outside of our shop, to which my husband responded, "Good, I can use more free publicity." Mario told them he had no intention of joining their Union and knew it was legal to work as a free man. The nastiness of their behavior scared me the most. Every night I would pace the floor of our house until I heard his knock at the door and I had him safe at home. The Union finally filed suit against him in East Brunswick Municipal Court.

  One of our new friends was an ex-FBI agent. He kept an eye on the shop and had the town police do drive-byes often for the security of workers and patrons of the establishment. Talking with a couple of his attorney clients, he questioned how anyone could stop a person from working and earning a good living. He prepared for court with his friend's help. On the prescribed day we were in court, his accusers were nowhere to be seen. Our attorney presented our facts and reasons why we thought the ordinance was illegal. The main argument: it prevented people from working at their trade on days when it would be most financially beneficial to their families. It took the judge about five minutes to deliberate and to declare the ordinance—

which had been passed during WWII in order to save electricity—unconstitutional, to the benefit and happiness of all people in the industry from then on. Another nice article in the newspapers as the first client on the next Wednesday was the mayor himself.

IV

We were earning enough to live a comfortable life and looking forward to many happy years, but as time went on, Mario became more and more morose again. During the week at work around people he was happy. The days he did not work, mainly Sundays and Mondays, he was miserable. Even our two daughters were not enough to make him happy. In Italy he had grown up with his extended family all living within a block from each other and most main meals were shared at his father's house. Here, some weekends, when it was just the four of us, he was not at all happy. Finally, I suggested we should try to move back to Italy and see if he could be happy there. I was ready to sacrifice myself and be away from my relatives. My parents were now living with my sister and brother-in-law in New Jersey. We were about 45-50 minutes away from them. So after much praying and thinking, the decision was made.

We bought three trunks, filled them with movable stuff, sold what little furniture we had purchased, and said our goodbyes to our American family and friends. For the second time I was parted from my husband. He stayed in New Jersey to take care of the business. I traveled to Italy on an ocean liner with my now five-year-old and baby of seven months. It took 11 days to reach our destination, Naples. During the trip we befriended other families. Among these were many Jewish families who at the time were returning to Israel to live on the kibbutz. My children and theirs got along well and spent a lot of time playing together. Their total belongings, like mine, were in just a few trunks. That group of travelers left the ship in Genoa, where they were to transfer to other means of travel to get them to Israel, their new Homeland. The way I saw the porters and baggage handlers treat their entire belongings made me cry: boxes and trunks were made to fall from high up, while people screamed in horror knowing how many precious personal belongings would not see their new homes safe and sound. I was appalled that my own countrymen, the Italians who had themselves so many migrant relatives, could do such things to other immigrants. From Genoa the ship stopped in my port of arrival, Naples. There too the handling of luggage was despicable. I cried and screamed in Italian, but the workers only shrugged and continued their behavior. I was happy finally to see the in-laws that had come to collect us. Tears of relief, pain, and gladness rolled down my cheeks all at once.

It takes about three hours from Naples to Campochiaro. We, of course, first stopped at the paternal home, which was up the steep street that led into the town of Campochiaro. The girls had to walk slowly up the incline—I had to carry the baby part of the way—in time, they would get used to the streets of this hilly town. My father-in-law again was very kind to us. So happy to see me and the children and ready to spoil all of us.

V

We were made comfortable in my sister-in-law's home. Her house was two blocks up from the father's house and one block in. It was a more recent building with brick walls on the outside; the inside was airy and more modern. The floors were all marble, but the walls were refinished with material like the one used in the US homes. On the first floor was a little entryway with two doors; the door on the left led to the kitchen—a spacious room with the usual fireplace in the front left corner with two chairs right at its side for those cold days in which one would need some warming up—a large table used as an island close to the window, a spacious pantry and four chairs along the length of the wall. The right door led to the large room with beautiful dining room furniture, above the table dangled a magnificent chandelier that my brother-in-law brought down from Rovello Porro where he had worked for the chandelier and lamps manufacturer. All the crystals they used came from Czechoslovakia and Bavaria. It also held a sofa, and a new television was added in the corner. Between the two doors was a marble stairwell that led straight up to the second floor.

On the second floor was the master bedroom, two smaller rooms and a spacious bathroom. The bathroom housed a footed bathtub to which a shower head was attached by a metal beam, a nice sink with bars on its side for towels and, of course, the toilet and the bidet. On the front of that room a long narrow window let in plenty of air. There was no separate shower and no shower curtain at first . . . we remedied that in time. The master bedroom had been made over to be our room. It was a large room with a matrimonial bed (sized between our queen- and king-size beds), a large armoire with both wooden and mirrored doors serving as the closet took up most of one large wall opposite the bed; and a French door that opened to a terrace overlooking the narrow street below. My lovely sister-in-law and husband moved into a smaller room. I was not there just for a weekend but expected to stay until after Mario joined us for the Christmas and New Year holidays, yet that is how generous they were. They were only too happy to accommodate the three of us.

Their two boys, 16 and seven years old, had a smaller room in which most of the storage had been kept, things like extra clothes, bed linens and towels in a hope chest and other trunks that were moved to another place for the time we were to stay. The family made do with less, so we could have more. That is the true Italian way: the love, the hospitality is an everyday affair.

My five-year-old turned six that September, and I enrolled her in the kindergarten. Because of her birth month, she was a little older than most in her class. She made friends with the other children easily. Of course, as a foreigner, she was a little bit the curiosity of her class. The children argued for her attention.

Everyone made a fuss over us. The town joined in the welcoming. Most people know each other and it seemed like a huge family. Especially when the baby fell down the marble stairs from the second floor. The word got out and many came to see if she was alright, if they could do anything to help. They brought her cookies and were truly concerned. This is how much of a family a town is in this region, not overly caring and familiar—just naturally Italian!

Saturday was market day. Early in the morning my young niece and I would venture out to do our shopping. From the 600 meters (1960 feet) above sea level, out the front door of the house was like stepping into a dream world. November gets chilly up in the mountains especially in the mornings. The early clouds, formed when the warm air from the valley below met the chilly air from the mountain tops, hung just below us. The whole valley was under cover; from the high vantage point it was like floating in the sky. The higher mountain peak, "il Matese," behind us was the one visible thing. It was both eerie and beautiful, still and very silent for about the hour it took for the clouds to dissipate and rise above us. Once we could see the road, my niece would drive us down to the neighboring open air market in Boiano. It is a wonderful way to live: fresh fruits, vegetables from the surrounding farms, along with clothing, shoes and anything one would need for the home—all at low prices with the possibility of haggling for the best discounts. The nearby boutiques also offered their fares at a decent cost. Always, the trip would end with a visit to the "bar," which is what their cafés are called, for a delicious pastry and a cappuccino or espresso—my mouth waters just at the thought.

VI

Christmastime neared and I wanted to decorate a tree for my daughters like we did in the US. Christmas trees were not the custom in this part of Italy. Friends actually had to get permission from the Forestry Patrol to cut one down for me. The Holy day was marked with Mass and then the finalization of the Christmas crèche, the nativity scene, whereby the youngest of the household would place baby Jesus in the manger. These nativity scenes in Italy are very beautiful and can get very elaborate. We had gone to the market in Naples, and I had purchased some figurines which I use to this day. In another neighboring town, we visited the famed nativity scene which took up a whole room and had many moving parts, based on what Bethlehem might have looked like at the time of Jesus' birth. This town was at about the same height as Campochiaro but on an even steeper incline on the mountain with the narrowest of road. It was a creepy drive just to reach this town of San Polo Matese.

It snows in that high mountain area and it gets very cold in the winter there. With a little help from us and the whole extended family, my brother-in-law had a propane gas stove installed in the space in the kitchen nearer to the dining room. The exhaust tube from the new gas stove to the chimney of the fireplace on the first floor provided more heating in the home where the floors and stairs were made of cold, if beautiful, marble. The downstairs doors to the stairwell were kept open for a couple of hours before bedtime in the hopes that some warm air would rise to the second floor and the bedrooms. We warmed the beds with the traditional brazier, a pan with a hinged lid and long handle, filled with tinder that would be passed over the sheets and then was left in the room to warm the air. We also used rubber hot-water bottles with almost boiling water in the bed. My two daughters and I shared the bed. Thankfully, I had brought the warm, footed PJs from the States for the three of us. By morning the water would start to freeze in the rubber bottles.

It was all OK until we would have to leave the warmth of our woolen blanket-covered bed. Then it was a mad dash to the bathroom and into warm clothing for the day. The knowledge that Mario would soon join us kept us going. Think of how those people lived for centuries with only their wood-burning fireplaces for heat. Still in the 1960s-70s, the little heat provided would make the stone walls "weep," as the moisture would build on the cold walls now being heated, even if a little.

To pass the time when nothing else was pressing, I put the children to preparing paper decorations for the anticipated Christmas tree, including a long garland of colored paper rings. My project, since all the women had works of embroidery, crochet or knitting, was knitting a sweater for my husband.

Mario arrived just after Christmas. The girls would not leave him for a minute, and I was ecstatic to have him with us again. He brought presents for the girls, a couple of dolls and candies they liked; for me, another warm PJ I had requested; more black pepper and perfume for all the ladies in the family. On my part, I proudly presented him with my gift, the knitted sweater. It looked very nice except . . . the sleeves were way too long for him. I miscalculated the centimeters in the pattern book I was following to the actual inches he wore. To all there is a remedy and I knew how to shorten those; so after a good laugh, he enjoyed the warmth of my gift.

It was good to have my husband back day and night. Funny how two can warm each other under the covers even in very cold weather.

Reunited with my husband we began making plans for our future. We returned to Rome, and the two of us looked at some areas just outside the capital that we thought would make a nice living place for our family—they were building new homes near the Via Appia, an ancient road, just south of the city. After all our experiences, we decided a city life would be better than the small village way of living. There would be more opportunity for work, education for us and our children. We got all the information we wanted and after a couple of days returned to our present home. We celebrated New Year's with the family and enjoyed the festivities in the town. In the square, they were selling the traditional foods of the season: lentils (for monetary gains in the new year); Baccala (cod which came to the town from far away, preserved in salt and needed three days to prepare); and the different dishes of pork (the pigs having been killed in late fall were now beginning to be cooked); of course, all accompanied by drinks of good wine, both the local and sparkling wines that were more often paired with some of the Panettone, traditional Italian bread, left over from Christmas.

VII

Early in January a phone call reached us from our attorney in New Jersey. There had been a break-in at the salon . . . except, he explained, the police said the window had been broken from the inside, and their suspicion fell on Mario's partner. Our attorney found out he was not on the level with us. He and his wife had been using the business to pay for some of their personal expenses, even their laundry costs and the maid she hired to clean their home, and yet the business taxes that had been due were not paid. He believed the duo wanted to run the business into debt blaming that on Mario's absence; they would then take it over without us and sell it to make a profit for themselves.

"If you don't return fast, you may lose everything," the attorney told us.

Needless to say my husband was on the next flight out to New York. Together with his attorney he confronted the partner and told him in no uncertain way he wanted him out. Discovered and humiliated, it took just a little money to buy him out. Then they proceeded to obtain time to pay what was due the tax department. Mario did not want to use further procedures against his one-time friend—always the kind person he was. He did not bring shame on the whole family, especially his friend's two young sons. It was decided that we would return and take up were we had left off. Time for me to repack the trunks and suitcases. It was another sad farewell, but inside I was not a little glad to be returning to the States.

The children and I returned on January 23, 1972. We rented an apartment in Lawrenceville for a short time while friends helped us find and finally actually buy a home in East Brunswick where the salon was located. I loved the house and it became a loving home for us. It was a raised ranch with lots of big windows, three bedrooms and an office, eat-in kitchen and a large living room and dining room all on the first floor. The raised ranch feature that I really loved was that half the basement area was above ground and provided for additional large, airy windows. We turned half of that floor into a nice playroom, a sewing room for me, and a TV area with a corner bar for entertaining. The other half of the downstairs, opposite the windows, housed a large laundry and storage area and a two-car garage. The large back yard was roomy enough for a play area, vegetable garden and fruit trees.

VIII

We now had a home of our own, a growing business and a growing family, yet one thing was bothering us. Our residency status was not resolved as yet. To all visible effects we were legal residents. We paid business and personal taxes, including income taxes for we had regular Social Security numbers given to us when we first came to work in the US. Then a letter came from the Immigration and Naturalization (I&N) department. Apparently, someone had questioned our legal resident status and the Office wanted our permission to look into the affair. Our attorney suggested that our old friend and ex-partner would be the only one who might want to harm us in that way. This proved to be so, even as it was hard to accept since his own father lived and died in the US for over 40 years as an illegal resident. It takes a lot of envy to behave that way; it took me a long time to finally really forgive.

Through a friend, we met a very important person in the I&N in Washington D.C. We explained all we had done to try and get our green cards on a continuing bases. We brought him all the documentation and letters we had sent to the different offices explaining our situation. He asked us more questions and looked everything over carefully, including our passports which showed how we had gone to Europe and Canada on many occasions and always freely returned home to New Jersey. He was stunned!

"I prepared many of the documents you filed to come back to the US myself—I would not have believed you took so many trips and was not stopped and questioned further." Then he broke into a laugh.

He made us understand this meeting was "off the record" as a friend and old classmate of our trusted attorney. We were told to go home and keep living within the law and bide our time. The immigration quotas currently in use were expected to be changed very soon—it would be a matter of a very few months—something Washington had been working on for some time. We would be informed through regular channels when that would occur and our status might be changed. More documents, including all information on our daughters, our home purchase, our business, and our employees' citizenship statuses information, had to be forwarded to the proper department.

The waiting game is difficult, but with new hope in our hearts we waited and prayed. After not a few sleepless nights news finally came. We were scheduled to go to the immigration offices on such-and-such a day in January 1973.

On December 30, 1972 I gave birth to our third daughter. This time—would you believe?—another different delivery. Baby No. 3 came early, at eight months. I was in full labor, and Mario drove me back to Princeton Hospital, yet in the middle of labor, when her head was already in the birth canal, the labor pains stopped. My body had decided that maybe it was not yet time, but it was too late. The baby's head was already in a point of no return, and Dr. Goldberg used forceps to help her into the world. Another lovely, beautiful girl. She was so small, little over four pounds. Her sisters were anxiously waiting for her, but she had to stay in the hospital nursery for a whole week before she was allowed home. The girls were not happy to see me come home without their baby sister. I went back and forth from East Brunswick to Princeton Hospital's nursery every day for five days as I was not allowed to stay overnight.

The day I finally brought Daniela home we had quite a party as the rest of the family came to visit with the new arrival. Her sisters loved her. The oldest would hold her gingerly and marveled at how small she was; the three-year-old behaved like a little mother—they shared a room—she had her real-live baby doll. She would not let me give her the bottle. It was her work, she said. They remained very close through the years. Years later my oldest admitted she was always jealous of her younger sisters. She felt left out, because she was alone in a room by herself while the other two shared a space. How wrong was I to think the older girl, by almost five years, would want to be in her own room, decorated just for her. It was too late—over 30 years later—when I learned how she had felt. There is nothing I can do now except encourage the three sisters to love and keep close to each other.

I was still recuperating from Daniela's birth, yet in early January we were on time for our appointment in Newark, New Jersey. I slowly made my way up the high flight of stairs to the second floor of the federal building that housed the I&N. The elevator was out of order that day. We were ushered into a large room full of expectant people. A few minutes after we signed in, our names were called. People had been waiting, some for over two hours, before us and looked at us suspiciously. In the inner office, the gentleman behind the desk rose and offered us our seats, and opening a folder he removed some documents. Our hearts were beating so loud I was sure he heard them. I held Mario's hand so tight I left nail marks in it. Then the face across from us broke into a nice smile as he handed us the documents and said, "Welcome to the United States," and rose to shake our hands. Relief, happiness, tears of joy as we looked at the green cards with our names on them that told everyone who wanted to know that we were now Legal Residents of this marvelous country. We could not stop thanking that clerk, and we hugged him before we were ushered again passed the waiting crowd and out the building free to join our American daughters in our happy home at last!

Unless you lived the experience, you cannot imagine what it is like to belong to one country or another and not really belong there—to be born somewhere and live somewhere else and love more than one country, not knowing which to call home. How lucky those that are born, live and die in their native land. How special the right to travel and visit other lands yet have the one home to come back to in freedom and peace. This was finally our status that day in January 1973: no more fears, no more nightmares, no more tears!

IX

The years passed, we were happy. We had a comfortable home, and our daughters were growing with only the minor children's problems. Donatella's teachers said she did not understand English, which was rubbish. I spoke only English to my girls, and they grew up watching English TV until we went to Italy in 1972. Truth was her ear passages were often plugged and she did not hear them speak to her. She was diagnosed with ever-recurring ear and nose infections. Then she had strep and came down with scarlet fever as a result of her allergy to the virus. Doctors recommended we have her adenoids removed and so we did back in Princeton. She progressed well in grammar school after that.

When you have children, you know they will be different from one another. Daniela was my little tomboy. She played with dolls only if she could take them, and really whatever other toy she had at the time, apart. She wanted to know how things worked and in that we encouraged her. Still, there were times when she was the perfect little girl. Later in life, school came easy to her. She never seemed to need to study or do much homework, and what had to be done was done very quickly, unlike her sister Sabrina who needed to study extra hard. We learned much later Sabrina had a form of dyslexia that made reading laborious.

We decided to adopt a dog when Daniela was six months old. Blaze had a pedigree; he was a beautiful tan and black German shepherd from a family of show dogs. His grandfather had won many medals and was on the cover of the German shepherd guidebook. The only reason Blaze could not compete was that he was too tall at the shoulders to be considered, but he was perfect to us. He fit in nicely with our family. My eldest daughter could do anything to the dog and he would not complain. The baby, he decided, was his duty to protect. Our house had an open stairway from the kitchen to the basement. I thought I needed a pet gate to keep the baby from falling down the stairs until the day I discovered I really did not need one. Every time she would head for the stairs, the dog got there first and placed himself across the way. My youngest would never be able to pass through or go around the ever-guarding pet. Then one day while we were all playing outside, Blaze darted across the street too fast for us to stop him. The car already on a slow drive, screeched to a halt—too late, the dog had been hit. The driver got out remorsefully repeating he did all he could; it was not his fault; he owned a dog of his own. We reassured the man, we had been only a foot away on the sidewalk, following and calling the dog back to us.

"Not your fault at all. Please calm down before you continue on home."

The shepherd was not too badly hurt, but he did spend the night at the vet's anyway. The next day my second born was so glad to have him home again she gave him a big hug. Blaze, caught off-guard and with his still aching head, reacted by biting her on her cheek. The two of them stood eye-to-eye in height and he just turned his head to nip her. She only needed one stitch, but for the next few days the dog cried whenever she was near. You could see how sad he was that he had hurt her. Friends and neighbors thought the dog should have been quarantined. We knew he was healthy and that he had only reacted out of pain and shock. From that day on they became best of friends. Now Blaze slept next to the girls' bedroom and not ours.

On a visit to Mario's cousins in College Point, New York, we talked about Mario's insomnia—he slept very few hours each night and still does—and how he would roam around the house disturbing the rest of us at night. Cousin Pietro was an artist. In the past, they had worked together on repairing and restoring some statues in their hometown church. Pietro asked Mario if he still liked to draw or paint. At first my husband complained he could not draw a straight line. To this our cousin said, "That is what rulers are for." Back home Mario started to paint and was much happier for he found out he did have talent and loved to use it. The rest of us were also happier with this arrangement. Any time he could not sleep, he would paint. His hobby grew and to this day he is an accomplished artist with works of art in the hands of collectors in many parts of the world.

My days were busy with the children, keeping my home clean and husband happy. I learned to love to cook now that I had access to many more recipes than those my parents used. I learned my husband's family way of cooking also, and so we mixed the Northern Italian with the Central Italian cuisine. The risotto (rice) dishes became pasta and butter often changed to olive oil and tomatoes.

X

Gardening also became an important pastime, with my fruits, vegetables and flowers growing easily in the fertile piece of land we called our own. One summer I decided to plant some asparagus along the back fence of the property. Now, for that, you need to dig a two-foot trench for the roots to be spread in. I did just that, and as I dug, I came upon a heap of empty clams and other seashells. After some research, we found that at one time—many, many, many years ago—the beach had not been far from Central Jersey with native people living there for years. We thought about speaking to someone about our find, but we feared that would bring curious sight seekers, so we kept it to ourselves. That is when I started feeling the presence of the friendly spirits of three Indians who became my family's guardians and home protectors.

When Sabrina and the dog had their incident, I woke up in a start that night and felt a weight pressing on the foot of my side of the bed. My eyes were opened, but I felt rather than saw the presence of three Indian figures, two standing and one sitting on the bed. Their kind eyes and demeanor told me not to be afraid. Without speaking, they let me know not to worry, that everything would be OK. This was repeated on a few occasions. Daniela fell down the metal back steps and again a couple of stitches were needed. Mario gave me a scare when, at a friend's picnic, he dove head first into the pool and hit his head on the bottom, where he stayed for a moment—long enough to scare us all.

"Please get him out of the water," I told my friend. I was frozen in place. I believed him already gone.

We stretched him next to the pool and slowly he came back to us. Don't you know, all such things always happen on the weekends when your doctors are not around? He refused an emergency room visit, slept flat on the floor that night . . . thankfully his doctor had ordered some pain pills over the phone. He would see him in the morning. Our physician couldn't believe he was still walking: his neck had been compressed by the dive and his body's weight. Stubborn Italian as he is, he was back at work attending to his clients' needs the next day. The first and only time I actually saw him take pills without grumbling, until much later in life when he went on the statins for his cholesterol. He recuperated slowly but surely and is still now working a few days a week behind the hairstylist chair. On both occasions my Indian guides came to visit me.

    Then again on the occasion of our big bout with the flu in 1974. The children brought the flu virus home from school; almost at once the three girls got sick. We first took care of our ailing daughters and then the daughters took care of us. Donatella was all of nine years old then and she took charge of our meds and looked after her younger sisters. The dog took care of them all. Blaze slept in the hallway by our bedroom doors and would not move except to eat or be let out when needed. He followed the children around like a good nanny. But I knew we would be all right thanks to the benevolent visits from my Native friends. For many years I felt the protective nearness of those three figures. People may not believe, but I know they were real and good and welcome in my home.

    Meanwhile, our business grew well—we helped one of our employees open his own salon and wished him luck in his venture—and our home was most comfortable, especially since it was close to anything one might wish for: grocery store, convenience store, churches, library, schools and even a shopping mall were within walking distance, if one wished; easy access to the NJ Turnpike to travel to New York City or Philadelphia; less than an hour from my sister Bianca;

and not more than eight hours to Montreal for family visits.

We put up an above-ground swimming pool in the back yard. The children loved it and so did we. Summers in New Jersey can be hot and humid; the pool helped the time pass easier then. On weekends, we also travelled to the seashore as often as possible. Long Beach Island was our favorite destination, especially Beach Haven. It took about one and a half to two hours, depending on the traffic, but the day spent on the sand and by the ocean made it worthwhile. Sometimes we would meet my sister and her family there. My parents loved the idea of swimming in saltwater again—this was much better than the Plage Ideal back in Montreal. One year we sisters got together and rented an apartment for one month just half a block away from the beach. We took turns using the apartment: two weeks my family stayed with my sister's family from Montreal; two weeks Bianca's family stayed with Giuliana's family. It was a wonderful way to spend our vacations, enjoying the special bond of sisterhood and letting the young cousins get to know each other more. I waited eagerly for the summers and those trips down the Shore.

My soul felt refreshed after every visit to the ocean. From Barnegat Light on the north of the island, which I managed to visit and walk up to the top, to Surf City with the wilder waves, Ship Bottom, and of course our favorite, Beach Haven, with its beach, shops, amusement park and restaurants, made life worth living there.

Mario had made some good friends and was happier this time around. For about six years all progressed well; we were mostly happy and contented. Then another idea was put in his head. Darn those well-meaning friends! Once one friend told him about California and how it had a lot of what the Italian Coast had to offer, every week someone else would regale him with their stories of visits to California, especially San Francisco.

"If you were to go there, you would stay there for sure," they taunted Mario.

So another dream took root in his heart.

XI

In 1978 we decided to visit this California so well-described by many friends. We would meet up with a friend of ours there. The girls were left in my oldest sister's care. Giuliana had come down from Montreal to stay with them, and Mario and I flew to San Francisco. Upon landing we went directly to the St. Francis Hotel. It was about four o'clock in the afternoon, and as we entered the lobby, we noticed that most women were wearing fur coats and scarves. Since it was August, we believed they must have been getting ready for a fashion show. The desk clerk asked us for a credit card. Mario was upset (we did not use credit cards at that time). We showed him the checks from American Express, which was our traveling funds. Luckily, our friend was already there. He vouched for us and treated us to a wonderful dinner and, in the morning, to breakfast. There was only one difference between him and us: he was an attorney who traveled on business with a nice business expense account, while our finances were much more limited. I did not particularly like going up in the glass-walled elevator that went up to the 27th floor and looked out over the city from the Union Square . . . beautiful but a little scary.

As nice as San Francisco is, it is cold and damp. In the morning, the fog covers the lower part of the city, like the fog clouds that hid the Italian valley in Campochiaro, and riding the open cable cars is fun if you are properly bundled up for the cold, i.e. those scarves and gloves were indeed most useful and necessary.

We started our sightseeing at Ghirardelli Square and Garden, lunched at Fishermen's Wharf and Market on the coast (you can spend much of a day just there), a trip on the cable cars brought us to the historical Telegraph Hill where the first telegraph communication tower was erected in 1849. From there signals went out to ships entering the Golden Gate area. We visited an

Italian restaurant and Chinatown and enjoyed the sites and the markets on the Hill. Bought some souvenirs for the family. On the last day we took a boat trip along the bay, passed under the Golden Gate Bridge and traveled around Alcatraz. How could anyone safely swim in those cold waters? Apparently, authorities do not believe any prisoners successfully made the escape. Legend, though, says that five escapees were unaccounted for and, who knows, they may have somehow reached terra ferma. The high-security prison was at one time home to famed mob boss Al Capone. It is now, since 1986, a national recreation area and a National Historic Landmark, but we could not visit the site due to ongoing work being done.

  It was odd to be so cold in August, so we decided to travel south. Our intent was to get to a warmer Los Angeles in a few days. Along the way, we visited Big Sur, a quaint village on the coast, and the Los Padres National Forest; marveled at the tall cliffs, but I cringed at the sharp turns in the road. I had been in tall buildings and walked in the Italian Alps at camp as a child, rode the Amalfi Coast twice, north to south and vice versa, and yet this one trip from San Francisco south gave me the jitters. From the East Coast of the USA, I could look out over the blue Atlantic and know other landmasses existed there; I visited some areas in Europe; I was born there and came across that ocean a number of times already; I knew the general locations on the world map, I was rather good at geography—at that moment though, from the high vantage point above those rocky Californian cliffs with the hairpin turns of US Route 101, my mind told me the world beyond that dark water DID NOT exist. That was the start of my fear of heights. I was very happy when we reached the more level area of the road.

We wanted to visit Hearst Castle in San Simeon, but the castle was being worked on and no tours were available. We continued south. At our next stop for refreshments, I realized my wallet was missing with my driver's license, green card and the American Express checks I was carrying. We were close to Santa Barbara and it was evening, so we decided to stop for a night and seek information the next morning.

Mario had his share of the travel checks; some of those paid for our overnight stay. The next morning we got up, ate breakfast and were greeted by a lovely view of the coast. We went to the American Express office and reported the loss and received the promise that the replacement checks would be there within the day. I reported the loss to the local police and to the New Jersey Motor Vehicles office. I also called the Immigration and Naturalization office and was told I needed to know the ID number that was on my green card so they could locate me in the system. This I did not have with me. I gave them all the information I could, including the date the card was issued and my husband's card number, thinking this should be enough to find my records. Apparently it was impossible to do anything else. I now knew why so many illegal aliens could not be found if they couldn't even find me. The police was more helpful: taking my information on the loss of these documents, I was given the paperwork to prove that the missing papers had been reported. All I could do was wait until I was back in New Jersey to renew my driver's license, get a copy of the green card and my insurance cards. Within the afternoon my new traveling checks had been issued and a stop payment put on the original ones—at least the banks were more efficient than our government offices.

That all done, we took time to visit this city we had stopped in. What a beauty! The coastline, the water, the different beaches and hills all around Santa Barbara reminded us of Italy and the Naples region much more than San Francisco. The climate was also much milder. We definitively liked it here more. There were colleges and universities in town and nearby. The Spanish influence in the architecture at the Paeseo and the downtown courthouse area, the many shops and good restaurants were a delight. I told Mario, "If we ever move West, this is where I want to come to." Here with the many terra cotta roof tiles, like in many towns in Italy, I could feel at home.

Next day we continued on to Los Angeles. We did not care for the sprawling city with the busy highway and the smog in the air. The tour to the movie actors' homes was about all we could do, since our plane left that afternoon. We were happy to return home to our children and our busy lives.

Another year, 1978, ended with the idea we would think about California for awhile.

XII

A short while it was indeed! Mario went to California again in early 1979 and on his return informed me he had made an offer to purchase a business and was ready to move. I was not totally unhappy, since the business was in Montecito on the outskirts of Santa Barbara. It is the richest area in Santa Barbara County; many actors and other wealthy people call it home. They may work in Los Angeles or Hollywood, but this is their hometown. Part of Montecito sits at the foothill of the Santa Ynez mountain range and goes down to the Pacific Ocean. Its many estates are mostly secluded by high walls and sturdy gates with an abundance of trees. Just on its west end is the city of Santa Barbara.

However, that is all I knew, and we still had not sold either our booming business or our house. In addition, I had planned a surgical procedure for that spring, so while we started packing and getting things ready, we talked to our attorney and accountant, both of whom tried to discourage us from selling everything. The business was progressing well and would be worth a good sum. They said we would miss our family and friends. Mario was unmovable. He had made up his mind and so it would be.

I had the children and my health to consider, so everything else did not encroach into my mind. We had moved before, that did not scare me. I thought we would get a nice return on our money from both the business and the house, so my courage was up. We packed with the help of my papà, mamma and sister Bianca. We took our farewell trip to Montreal to see our relatives and explain our decision. Mario's cousins in College Point were sad to see us go again. They had helped us when we returned from Italy in 1972. They even gave us a car that they had intended to sell and a couple of kitchen items to use until our trunks had come back. I still have the aluminum frying pan our cousin gave me. (I keep what reminds me of the love I shared with others and they with me; it brings me comfort and hope that life will continue well for our family.)

A good buyer was found for our house. I think my heart hurt a little as I showed the new owner all that we loved about our piece of land and our comfortable home. Friends and neighbors helped us fill the moving truck, which Mario and his nephew had decided to drive to our new home in the West. The truck sat almost completely full on our driveway waiting for the day. Then on a day like any other Mario came home all exited with the news that he had sold the salon to one of his employees . . . for $10,000. I thought I would faint!

"What? Just $10,000? What can we do with that?" The accountant said it was worth about four times that at least. He told us how to figure the price according to how much business we did in a year. "You didn't even ask me!" I was furious at him, but I was never able to really have a fight with him.

In Mario's mind he had built the salon, it was his baby. Without him it was not worth more. Such ego! What had I contributed to the success....nothing?! I just kept his home, his children, did the books and the running around. Yes, it was true, I did not cut hair or even go to the shop often, but I felt used, abused and very, very hurt. At that moment my blood boiled and my heart pounded loudly. Because my parents were temporarily visiting to help with the move and I had that medical appointment at the hospital, I tried not to show the hurt and the disappointment too much. What could I do? The huge truck was full and ready in front of the house. The house was sold. Everyone was excited about the coming trip. Me—I was so angry! I felt hatred for the husband I had loved so much. Yes, I truly hated him at that moment. I moved about like a zombie just waiting for the time we were leaving.

The following day I was at the hospital early in the morning to prep for the surgery, a tubal ligation, that was supposed to be over in a few minutes and as easy as pie, so the doctor had told me. I would be back home in a day. Good, I told him, because we were ready to leave town in two weeks' time. No one noticed that

I was actually shaking; the nurse kept reassuring me not to worry, it was an easy procedure that was done many times over every day. They thought I was nervous because of the operation, and I told no one exactly how I felt. Could I tell them that I was wondering whether I would stay with my husband or even move with him or tell him to go by himself? Could I really say that I did not love him anymore? That he had hurt me so very much? How little he valued me to not even ask my opinion before he sold what we had built together over the past seven years? Was that really what he believed, that I did not count? That the home and family I cared for did not help his success? Now I knew how women felt and why so many people divorced. Would I be the next one to say goodbye to a marriage that started with so much love?

The operation was at 7:00 a.m. the next morning. I was ready, I thought, for it all to be done and over. My nurse said I would be in the recovery room soon and back into my regular room for a short time thereafter. I woke up in the recovery room and from the coming and going around me sensed something was awry. The clock showed that I had been asleep for over three hours. That was not the short time expected. I questioned the young intern that was taking my vitals and was told that I had apparently suffered a heart attack during the operation.

"What?!" I screamed, "How could that be?" But even as I questioned them I thought I knew the answer.

Now the medications they gave me kept me calm, much calmer than I wanted to be.

I was wheeled into a private room, and there my husband and my mother told me how worried they had been and finally relieved to see me OK. The next day my parents returned to visit, my husband had to work until the evening. My parents and I were speaking in Italian and another patient, hearing us, came into the room to say hello. He turned out to be an immigrant born and raised in Trieste, our old hometown. We all became instant friends. He was there for his heart valve transplant and said he would be home in a couple of days in Milltown, a few miles from our home in East Brunswick.

"I don't believe your heart attack," he kept saying. "You are much too young and pretty."

Silly, I know, but the compliment perked me up.

The doctors wanted to perform a newly devised test to see the damage done to the heart system, angioplasty had just lately been used. My girlfriend, Liselotte, called to wish me well but said I should refuse the procedure. She had read all about it and said it was too soon, too new, and that people had been hurt and even killed by the performance, that it was all in the news. After discussing it with my doctor, I decided to put that on hold for now. I had to get home to my daughters and to my unsure future. Against his best advice, the surgeon agreed only as long as I would promise to take the medication he prescribed, nitroglycerin. Nitro, as it was called, would have to be carried with me always just in case.

"You need to take a pill anytime you feel your heart behaving funny."

Back home I was too busy with the packing, Mario was busy with the transfer of the business and the truck packing, no time to even think about much else. At times my heart frightened me with palpitations and I would immediately lie down and put a pill under my tongue. That seemed to calm me . . . now I know that the stress would have calmed just by my laying down and letting others do the work needed. I thought, I must live for those three wonderful children. My parents decided they would travel with me to California and help with the move and the girls. Mario felt reassured that I would have their support, and soon he was ready to leave. With his nephew, he drove the truck with our belongings to Santa Barbara and waited until the six of us flew out to join them.

Talking to my close friend and family I decided to visit my old doctor in Princeton for his opinion on my health prognosis. Upon hearing the story of my "heart attack" this doctor was amazed. Immediately he ordered his assistant to give me an EKG (electrocardiogram test). It did not show any sign of a heart problem. He asked if the surgeon had been made aware of my slight heart murmur. I said it must have been in my medical records.

"I don't believe you had a heart attack at all," this doctor said. "With your heart murmur and your excited, nervous state, I believe all you had was a valve prolapse," and went on to describe what that was. "The first thing to do is to throw away the nitroglycerin. That could kill you because you don't need it. When you get to Santa Barbara go see my friend, a brilliant cardiovascular doctor, who can confirm what I just told you. Keep calm until then and enjoy your new hometown." He had visited his old classmate there many times—he make sure I had his friends' business card before I left his office—and knew I would love living in California. I was relieved yet still skeptical and did not get rid of the nitroglycerin just then. I brought it with me to Santa Barbara, just in case.

XIII

Mario, our nephew, truck and all got to California in three days and stayed at a motel to wait for us. The girls, my parents and I flew to Los Angeles. My husband met us at LAX, and we drove from there to Santa Barbara. The short ride, 90 miles to the beautiful city, was uneventful. The girls were very excited, and my parents, tired as they were from the trip, just kept looking at the scenery and marveled at the vision of palm trees and the hills on one side and the Pacific Ocean on the other. I felt odd: I was tired, yes, from the move and the plane trip; my heart was pounding harder and I took one of the pills I was carrying, just in case; while my husband told us of the exciting way they had made it to the coast and the possibilities he saw in our future—I just wondered if we had a future. Would I be able to find love for him still in my aching heart? Could I trust in him again? I looked at my three beautiful children and prayed it would all come out all right.

That same afternoon we were shown a house to rent that was large enough for the seven of us to live in. Three bedrooms, two baths, a nice kitchen, dining room and large living room with a gas fireplace. From the high hill it was on, we had a sliver of view of the ocean. After deciding we could afford it, the lease was signed. The next few days were busy moving our stuff into the house on Manitou Road. We met some of the neighbors. The girls were happy there were children their age around us to play with. The two boys next door became good friends and their parents were wonderful neighbors. On the north side, our neighbors were the dean of students and her husband, a professor, at the Santa Barbara City College, again wonderful people. Other college professors lived nearby with their family. Across the street lived a lovely family with a girl the age of our oldest and a couple of business people whom we came to know and appreciate as close neighbors. Down the end of the street John Travolta moved his mother in; we did not meet her but saw her a few times outside her home.

Many of the residents in the city were transients either by choice—people that wanted a change of scenery—or those who were transferred from jobs in other parts of the country, and those who were trying to see if the promise of golden opportunities came true in the fabled West Coast. Our family fit in with all three of those, I believe, so we settled in this new adventure.

We worked our salon and had most interesting clients, among which a few actors who called Montecito/Santa Barbara home. Some lived or worked close enough to walk or bike to our place. The actors who worked in Hollywood but made Santa Barbara home were living here as regular people. Away from their homes they would be stopped, harassed and bothered; here they were our neighbors, just people living their lives as quietly as possible. We never even asked for their autographs (I now sometimes wish we had). The problem we faced was with our employees, especially beauticians. The California lifestyle was hard to live with. One would have a fully scheduled day but would call in late in the morning with, "It's a beautiful beach day, not coming in" or "Too much partying last night" or often the drug usage made it impossible for a good work ethic. As soon as enough money to pay their rent was earned, no need to work further. After a few infuriating months, we knew we could not keep going with this business.

We met a woman, Ann, who talked to us about opening an Italian restaurant. She would provide the financials needed and stay as a silent partner. Our nephew, with restaurant experience, was willing to join us from New Jersey. After consulting with an attorney and our bank, we incorporated and started the hard work of running and working a restaurant. People kept telling my husband to make it a pizzeria—easy money—but he insisted a fine-dining establishment is what he wanted. So we worked it, often 12-14 grueling-hour days. The only fly in the ointment was the never-easily-obtainable, promised moneys from our partner. Until the day after some more checking by our banker and attorney, we all realized that our silent partner was an excellent con who duped us, as well as at least two attorneys and the banks who lent her large sums of money, into believing her story of financial wealth. It was then disclosed she had very little, if any, money. She used the "owner of a restaurant" as her screen to meet and dupe other businesspeople into lending her money. Because she was a well-endowed and pleasant-looking woman, she was able to trick not a few men into her scheme of things. She would bring men into the restaurant and expect them to pay her way, at a discount, of course, as a part owner. It took a bit of doing and another bit of money to legally get rid of her. Thank God we did, for not long after, her many suitors, attorney and bank tried to get satisfaction from us. But our legal counsel took care of keeping us out of more trouble.

Without her promised financial backing—she simply evaporated from Santa Barbara— there was no way we could continue holding on to our business. So we closed down and licked our wounds, so to speak.

XIV

Mario found part-time work in a men's hairstyling place and looked for other ways to earn a living. He got discouraged and felt responsible, even though he never really talked about that part of his feelings. He started to mope, and I could sense a serious depression coming on him. My parents, who after coming with us because of my health, had stayed to help us: when we had the restaurant, they came in after the children left for school to prep the food for the daily cooking; and after the closure of that business they even helped a little financially, with what little their Social Security was, just for one month. My mother kept telling me that I could get a job and bring in a wage. I knew from others' experiences that if I would contribute enough, then my husband might feel he did not need to earn more. With a depression started, the fact of not being the bread winner—that was a big pride booster—he could easily fall into deeper problem and lose the spirit to fight. So I told him that as soon as he got more work, I would look for a way to help him. Within the week he had managed to get something else to do. We took jeans and denim jackets from a friend who manufactured them in Los Angeles and sold them at the swap meet in town on the weekends. This we did for a while, with my parents watching the children, and it helped. Then luckily Mario was offered the position of manager at the posh restaurant in the Holiday Inn in Carpinteria, just a few miles down the coast from us. The Top of the Harbor revolving restaurant on the top floor of the Inn was a very nice restaurant that needed some strict control both in employee behavior and theft, especially with the kitchen and its pantry. The hours were long, but he loved it. He once again had contact with a lot of people: employees, customers and a few of the artists that came to perform at the venue and then ate at his restaurant. He went to work happily and liked what he was doing, and was thanked by his bosses for the great job he had done there.

Until then, Mario and I went about our daily chores as if nothing had happened. With all the hard work and long hours he never questioned, if he even noticed, my icy responses to his lovemaking. We were so preoccupied elsewhere in our lives that the loving part of our marriage did not phase us.

At that time also I was offered a job by my neighbor, the dean of students at Santa Barbara City College, and went to work at the Admissions Office with her. We would often walk the approximately 1.6 miles to work. I liked my job there. In the office we worked with the huge computers and did the data entry for the students' in-coming registration documentation and continuing scholastic records. We dealt with the students and their problems that related to our office. Working for and interacting with the youngsters kept us all young. It was the early years with computing and I liked the technology.

After two years there, I was given the responsibility of taking over the enlisting and registration for the spring semester. It was a challenge I undertook willingly and completed well, giving my co-worker, who was the head of that job for many years, the needed time off to re-coop from a surgery.

The College with manicured park-like grounds, sits on a cliff above Shoreline Drive and Leadbetter and West Beach. It was a real pleasure to have to go to work there each day. Water is my soul's element and this spot, looking over the Pacific, was perfect for meditating and healing.

Slowly the hatred in me subsided, and with deep thought and prayers I believed the marriage could continue and even one day be a happy one again, even for me. Every night I would join my spouse in our bed praying that this was the night I would feel love for him again . . . slowly, very slowly I started to at least get away from the hatred I had felt. I remembered the reasons I had fallen in love with this man in the first place: his love and respect for my parents, my family and his; the care he had for his daughters; the respect and love he earned and gave to friends and acquaintances; the effort he made, even with a cost to his Italian pride, to find work and earn a living; his belief that with faith and hope things would get easier. Slowly I allowed myself the luxury of learning to love again. Yes, deep down the heart was mending; the sun kept shining in beautiful Santa Barbara; love came creeping around the corner of my soul, and I could get lost again in those deep, dark eyes that belonged to my man.

There would be more ups and downs, easy hills and steep crevasses, but with love my life would continue to be a full one indeed.

END

Epilogue

Santa Barbara is a piece of heaven on hearth but not easy to live in. For many reasons we decided to move back East just before our fifth-year stay. With our three daughters, we drove back to Jersey in just three days. Yes, daughters, furniture and all again!

The story of our new back-to-the-East life I will leave for another time. Suffices to say that we spent the next 25 five years in East Brunswick, NJ, until we moved again… this time south to beautiful Florida to be close to two of our three daughters and their families.

A very special thank you to my daughter Sabrina Della Penta for all the hours editing this memoir.

And to all my family and friends who helped jog my memory—Grazie Mille!

Mario and I hope to make it truly a permanent home in beautiful St Augustine. I am again close to the beach and still dream of the other land I called home that still sings to me from across the ocean.

List of Photographs

1. Gisella Steffè   73
2. Giovanni Steffè   73
3. Nonna Piccia, Giovanna Starz Steffè   74
4. Nonno Natale Steffe   75
5. Nonna Grande, Margherita Zucca Steffè   76
6. My eldest sister, Giuliana Steffè   76
7. Guerino, Elise and Francesco Steffè   77
8. Nadia Steffè and kindergarten friend Brunetta   78
9. School Picture   79
10. SS Skaubryn   80
11. Gatekeeper' house on Montebello Estate   80
12. Side gate on Montebello Estate   81
13. Giovanni, Gisella and Steffè family   81
14. Bianca and Nadia Steffè   82
15. Steffè family at Montebello Estate   82
16. Mr. Cassidy's 4th Grade   83
17. St. Joseph of Rosemont Hospital   84
18. Patients at Rosemont Hospital   85
19. Steffè family in 1959   85
20. Giuliana Steffè and Angelo Pivetta   86
21. Giuliana and Angelo Pivetta's wedding photo   86
22. With friends at the Italian Radio station   87

23. Nadia Steffè in one of the Italian Club's performances	87
24. Plage-Ideale	88
25. Plage-Ideale with my friend Angelo	88
26. Bianca and Fred Procaccini's wedding day	89
27. My first trip to Princeton, New Jersey	89
28. Mario Della Penta performing	90
29. Mario Della Penta publicity photograph	91
30. Nadia and Mario Della Penta's our wedding day	92
31. Mario and Nadia in Piazza San Marco	93
32. The home where Nonna Piccia once lived	94
33. Venetian architecture in Capodistria	94
34. Serafina and Donato Della Penta	95
35. Antonio Della Penta and Pasquale Iannarella	96
36. Donato Della Penta and Mario Della Penta	97
37. Lower Campochiaro	97
38. Landmark Tower in Campochiaro	98
39. Pompeii	98
40. Vic Vannelli at Gentleman's Choice	99
41. Advertisement for Gentleman's Choice	99
42. Donatella Della Penta and friend	100
43. Our first house in New Jersey	101
44. Sabrina and Donatella Della Penta	101
45. Angelo and Giuliana Pivetta and family	102
46. Bianca Procaccini's family	102
47. Daniela Della Penta's christening	103
48. Giuliana Pivetta, Bianca Procaccini and Nadia Della Penta	103
49. Captain's Night	104
50. Ghirardelli Square	104

51. Alcatraz   105
52. Nadia and Mario Della Penta in Santa Barbara   105

Made in the USA
Middletown, DE
16 September 2018